REAL ALCHEMY

A Primer of Practical Alchemy

ROBERT ALLEN BARTLETT

PREFACE BY
BRIAN COTNOIR

FOREWORD BY
DENNIS WILLIAM HAUCK

IBIS PRESS
Lake Worth, FL

Published in 2009 by Ibis Press
An imprint of Nicolas-Hays, Inc.
P. O. Box 540206
Lake Worth, FL 33454-0206
www.ibispress.net

Distributed to the trade by
Red Wheel/Weiser, LLC
65 Parker St. • Ste. 7
Newburyport, MA 01950
www.redwheelweiser.com

First Edition 2006 by Quinquangle Press
Second Revised Edition 2007 by Lulu.com
Third Revised Edition 2009 by Ibis Press

Library of Congress Cataloging-in-Publication Data
available upon request

ISBN 978-0-89254-150-8

Cover painting by Benjamin Vierling
www.bvierling.com
Cover design by Studio 31
www.studio31.com

Printed in the United States of America

REAL ALCHEMY

Contents

KIDS! DON'T TRY THIS AT HOME!

The practice of Real Alchemy is inherently dangerous. Formal laboratory training is encouraged. Consulting a licensed physician is encouraged before consuming herbal preparations. Familiarize yourself with the laws that may apply to you in your jurisdiction and act accordingly.

Read as many of the other books on the subject of Alchemy as possible. (A list of recommended books can be found in the Bibliography.) Learn as much as you can from a qualified teacher. And above all, know the theory before attempting the practice.

This book is sold for informational purposes. The author and publisher will not be held accountable for the use or misuse of the information in this book.

by Brian Cotnoir

(Author of *The Weiser Concise Guide to Alchemy*)

As sentient, self-aware beings we have been engaged in the quest for *more*, the quest for *better* and the quest for *perfection* since we first stood upright and uttered our first words. To take what has been given to us and transform it, hoping and praying for the better, lies at the heart of what has been called *The Royal Art*, *The Way of the Philosopher*, or simply *The Art*, that is—alchemy.

The art and science of alchemy has been found throughout many times and regions. We can speak of Chinese alchemy, Indian alchemy, Hellenistic, Arabic and European. Some have focused on matter, some have focused on soul and others have a double focus on body and soul. As such, alchemy is not a smooth monolithic system, but rather a journey full of contradictions, false turns and dazzling insights into the worlds of creation. At times it seems to defy a single definition. But, in its most general, all-encompassing form, we can say with some degree of confidence that alchemy is the art and science of bringing something to its final perfection. That "something" may be corporeal or incorporeal and the processes involved are those of dissolution and composition.

The Greeks called alchemy *chemia*. They also used the words *chrysopoeia* and *argyopoeia*, literally gold-making and silver-making respectively. The *poeia* part of the word means *make* or *compose*, it is where we get our English word *poetry*. In Plato's *Symposium* Socrates recounts how the philosopher Diotima, while instructing him, once said: "There is poetry, which, as you know, is complex and manifold. All creation or passage of non-being into being is poetry or mak-ing, and the processes of all art are creative; and the masters of arts are all poets or makers." And just as music is composed out of the elements of sound and silence, and poetry out of elements of words and letters, so the art of alchemy is composed out of elements—the elements of matter and soul. And so, with its basis in the material, alchemy could be considered the poetry of matter. We follow the rules of composition, working with the elements, as in music or in language.

What are the elements of alchemy? In general the alchemists and philosophers speak of four elements—*Fire, Air, Water, Earth,* or of three principles—*Mercury, Sulphur, Salt.* The main processes are dissolution and composition. "If you do not skin the bodies of their corporeal nature and if you do not give a corporeal nature to incorporeal beings, then nothing you wait for will take place." Hermes shows here the heart of the alchemical process—the change of something into its opposite, and of taking apart and putting back together again. Maria the Jewess, one of our mothers of alchemy, alluding to Hermes, elucidates the role of opposites in the act of creation when she says, "Make the corporeal incorporeal and the incorporeal corporeal, join male and female and you shall have what you seek."

Alchemy can be understood as the release of soul from the body and its subsequent reunion with it. This is the essence of the secret of composition. And it is in the composing that we find the final perfection—and the key to this final perfection comes from us—as we read in the *Liber de compositione alchimiae,* where the monk Morienus answers Khalid ibn Yazid, "this matter comes from you, who are yourself the source, where it is found and whence it is taken ..."

Alchemy is said to be physical or spiritual—but the fact is, it is both. It has not always been practiced as both. There have been alchemists who dispensed with the "superstitions" of magic squares, planetary rulerships, etc. to focus on their dialog with matter. And there were others who have focused on the uplift of their soul, leaving behind the dross of alembics, retorts and furnaces. Each aspect is like seeing with one eye, each correct and accurate on its own. But yet, there is more. We have all seen 3D viewers that take two photographs, each offset by a bit that when viewed, pop into three dimensions. The split between the physical and spiritual interpretations of alchemy are like this: each photograph is accurate and complete and can stand on its own, as can each interpretation of alchemy. But it is when we put them together that the almost magical experience of three dimensions occurs, something more than each eye alone could imagine. Is this what the alchemists thought? Not in all cases, but alchemy is the richest when it is seen with both eyes. Listen to how Zosimos of Panopolis expresses this unity of the work in a letter to his sister:

> Let your body rest, calm your passions, resist desire, pleasure, anger, sorrow, and the dozen fatalities of death. In thus conducting yourself you will call to you the divine being, and the divine being will come to you, he who is everywhere and nowhere …
>
> Operating in this manner you will obtain the proper, authentic, and natural tinctures. Make these things until you become perfect in your soul.

Much has been written on the psychological and spiritual aspects of alchemy, but it is the physical aspect with its variety materials and processes that causes confusion and puzzlement. What is actually done in physical alchemy? Simply put, alchemy begins with the body, it begins with the material, begins with the here and now. As Morienus says, referring to the materials of the Great Work, "I will both bring before you the things called by these names, that you may see them, as well as work with them in your presence…. Do not depart from that which I have set forth for you and shown you, for you will go astray." And it is in this tradition that Robert Allan Bartlett in *Real Alchemy* shows the how and what of alchemy.

Please, know that these practices and materials are very real, and there is risk in this work, just as in chemistry. But with the necessary precautions, for those who do venture forth, there is real wisdom to be found. When this practice is joined with the intent to heal or something positive, things happen.

Start slowly and mindfully, put consistent effort behind the work and go through a few of the processes at a time. The basics are here, but reach into the primary sources from which these practices come and read them against your own practice and results. Dig into it, ask questions of the matter at hand, investigate it and not timidly. Soon you will clearly see that it is not a metaphor for something else, but rather that alchemy is fundamentally about transmutation in the physical world—of change from poison to medicine, from sickness to health, poverty to wealth, and ignorance to wisdom.

Ultimately, what you bring to the practice is where alchemy begins.

Istanbul, Turkey
Ramazan, 2008

Real Alchemy

FOREWORD by Dennis William Hauck

The book before you is an amazing accomplishment in many ways. My friend and fellow alchemist Robert Bartlett has laid bare the secret processes and experiments of our discipline with exceptional clarity and openness. He has exposed the Hermetic origins of alchemy and shown how modern alchemists approach the ancient art. But first and foremost, his book is a revelation of the genuine craft of alchemy as it was meant to be practiced.

While the work of Carl Jung and others have underscored the archetypal power and universal significance of alchemical symbols, alchemy itself is much more than a psychological commentary on the nature of the human psyche. It is true that alchemy reflects the highest aspirations of the human soul, for our gold has always symbolized the hastened perfection of Man as well as matter. However, any alchemist worth his salt knows that lasting transformation only takes place when the work is accomplished on all levels of reality – the mental, the spiritual, and the physical. The Great Work is actual work to be done with the hands, the heart, and the soul, and not just understood with the mind.

A medieval alchemist brought back to our era would be highly amused at the endless discussions among modern theorists as to the nature and depth of alchemy or its sudden blossoming in the offices of psychiatrists and New Age counselors. "Has no one ever tried it?" he would ask incredulously. "What good is such understanding without its practical application in the world?"

No alchemist in history ever thought the Secret Art was solely a mental discipline. The work of transformation takes place in the real world. Yet alchemy is not chemistry. Chemistry is a superficial science that deals only with the external forms in which the elements manifest. A chemist seeks to rearrange atoms and molecules to exhibit different properties of the same dead material. An alchemist seeks to create an entirely new substance by exposing its essences, bringing them alive, and causing them to grow.

When an alchemist performs a laboratory experiment, it is the culmination of careful planning to find the right timing and personal purification to create the sacred space in which the transformation can take place. The alchemist becomes an ingredient in his own experiment, and his intention and passion contribute to the outcome. He suffers as the essences are teased and tortured from the substance, and he is elated when the hidden spark of truth brings the dead matter back to life on a new level of being.

Admittedly, this is a strange way of looking at laboratory work in a materialistic, industrialized world, and there are many prejudices the modern mind must overcome to accept the possibility that alchemy is real. Yet perhaps, after reading this book with a free heart and open mind, you might find an ancient voice speaking to you through the drone of appliances, engines, and commercial broadcasts that make up our environment. The voice will whisper: But have you tried it?

Dennis William Hauck is an author, consultant, and lecturer working to facilitate personal and institutional transformation through the application of the ancient principles of alchemy. As one of the world's few practicing alchemists, he writes and lectures on the universal principles of physical, psychological, and spiritual perfection to a wide variety of audiences that range from scientists and business leaders to religious and New Age groups. He is the editor of the *Alchemy Journal* and on the board of directors of the International Alchemy Guild. His bestselling books include *The Emerald Tablet: Alchemy for Personal Transformation* (Penguin Putnam 1999), and *The Sorcerer's Stone: A Beginner's Guide to Alchemy* (Citadel Press, 2004).

PREFACE

These days the word **Alchemy** is lumped together with psychic phenomena, ghost hunters, UFO sightings and other "Dark Arts." Everyone has heard of such things but only a few know more of the details, especially those concerning alchemy.

A few years ago, my wife was in a class for Hypnotherapy certification and she happened to mention that I had an interest in alchemy. Everyone was intrigued. They asked if I would be willing to give a two or three-hour presentation on the subject.

My hesitant reply was, "Yeah, I can do that." That first time, I talked for five hours. People were entranced and asked if we could have another class to continue. Before I could finish constructing an outline for the second class, I received a call asking if we could make the whole presentation three six-hour classes.

Since then, I've been teaching the classes each year. There is a real thirst out there for information on the practical alchemical arts.

This book is something of a transcription from those classes and will provide a short primer for those interested in exploring firsthand the "Sacred Science and Royal Art" which is alchemy.

REAL ALCHEMY

Now I will teach and describe the secret of the arts, which secret is at the heart of all secrets hidden in the art of alchemy; since one will here understand the wonderful works that God has accomplished in all things he has made out of the four elements... For I shall here teach you to know the spirits of herbs, trees, and all growing things; how to separate them from their bodies, and also how to purify the four elements and restore them to their first being and their perfect power; that is, that when the elements are purified, how they can be put together again and make a perfect and fixed body of them, which is then glorified and has a miraculous effect.

— Issac Holland, *Opera Vegetabilia* (15ᵗʰ century)

INTRODUCTION

Practical Alchemy

When we mention the word *"Alchemy,"* most people think that means a now-discredited method of turning lead into gold.

Then we have the psychologists, after Jung, who tell us that alchemy, with its fantastic imagery, is only a metaphor -- that is to say, that alchemy is an allegory describing the processes of psychological reintegration. Many believe this is the new and correct interpretation of the alchemists' riddle. It's all Psychology.

Yet, if we look into the lives of the alchemists themselves we find they were indeed involved in laboratory work that appears to be similar to what we call chemistry today.

Alchemy has been described by many of the ancient masters as a sort of "Celestial Agriculture." I like that definition.

It is amazing that alchemy, once called the Divine Art or Sacred Science, has fallen into such obscurity that it is now only remembered as the primitive beginnings of modern chemistry. And yet, alchemy lies at the root of every Western Esoteric tradition as well as many of the arts and sciences, including medicine and pharmacology. Alchemy has been called "The Mother of all Science and Wisdom."

In a nutshell, alchemy is an ancient Art and Science concerning the Mysteries of Life, of Consciousness and its Evolution.

7

Currently there are many people who latch on to the word alchemy and attach it to any number of "New Age" transformative tools (such as alchemical massage or alchemical hypnotherapy) because alchemy is associated with the transmutation or transformation of something of little worth into something of great value.

In the following pages, we're going to explore alchemy -- the *Real Alchemy*. This means we will be exploring Practical Laboratory Alchemy. We will include here the history, theory, and simple practices that anyone can use to prepare herbal and mineral extracts in the ancient tradition.

Who am I? And where is this information coming from? I've been exploring alchemy since I was about twelve years old. I've had a laboratory of my own in one form or another since even before then.

In 1974 I began an intensive study of alchemy at the Paracelsus Research Society (PRS) -- later called Paracelsus College and located in Salt Lake City, Utah. The classes were taught by Dr. Albert Reidel, who preferred to be known as Frater Albertus.

Frater Albertus was one of the most well-known practical alchemists of the twentieth century. He also taught classes in Germany, Switzerland, New Zealand and Australia.

The classes took place on a small campus composed of a dormitory, a lecture hall, and a laboratory. Class size was limited to twelve students and contact with the outside world was not encouraged (no radios, TV, phones, or newspapers) so the student could fully immerse himself in the teachings. It was a Mystery School.

The classes ran Monday through Saturday, from 9 A.M. to 5 P.M. (with homework and lab work that ran continuously) for two weeks each year over seven years. At the end of each two-week class, the students were given work to accomplish in preparation for the next year's class.

By 1976, I decided to return to a university where I could finish my degree in chemistry in hopes of one day working at Paralab -- the commercial offshoot of the PRS that would be opening soon.

Paralab offered a line of herbal and mineral preparations formulated along alchemical principles for research and alternative healthcare practices.

After graduation in 1979, I was appointed Chief Chemist at Paralab and remained in that position until its closure in late 1983. Frater Albertus passed away in 1984.

I have been a professional Chemist since that time and have worked on my own projects through the years.   Being employed as a research and analytical chemist has allowed me to collect state-of-the-art analytical data on many products from alchemical experiments, and so begin to answer some of the questions modern science would ask concerning these materials.

Frater Albertus had a simple definition of what alchemy is about. He said that alchemy was about Evolution and "Raising the Vibratory Rate."   To understand that correctly requires some understanding of natural laws and some introduction to mysticism or occult philosophy.

The information being taught here is an ageless wisdom handed down for centuries by an oral tradition and later in a necessarily obscure language and symbolism. It is called the Hermetic Philosophy, after its legendary founder Hermes Trismegistus -- the Greek name for the Egyptian god Thoth (god of wisdom and inventor of all science and magic.) The ancient sages often referred to themselves as the "Sons of Hermes" or the "Sons of Wisdom."

The   earliest   descriptions   of   alchemy   link   it   to transformations in matter through the influence of light or spirit, or fire. It is the metamorphosis of matter orchestrated by spirit.

It is generally agreed that ancient Egypt is the birthplace of alchemy (as it is known in the Western World) and it is there that we begin our exploration.

CHAPTER ONE

A Brief History of Alchemy

The origins of alchemy are lost in history and theories abound as to where it might have originated:

- God taught it to Adam and later to Moses.
- Fallen Angels taught it to human women in exchange for sex.
- It is a remnant of lost Atlantean technology.
- Extraterrestrials taught it to our ancestors.

Whatever its true origin is, recorded history documents an esoteric tradition that has existed for several thousand years.

Mystery and magic permeate all that is ancient Egypt. From beginning to end, Egypt has been called a theocratic state, ruled by a very powerful priesthood. The priesthood was divided into various castes, each with specific duties -- such as scribes and astronomers. Of special interest to us are the priests, who worked with materials in ways we might describe today as chemistry. These priests, often working under an oath of secrecy regarding their art, developed skills in metallurgy, ceramics, medicine, mummification, and winemaking, to name just a few.

The study of the operative forces at work in the universe was the primary goal of the priesthood. They called these forces the "Neteru" from which we obtain our word, "Nature." The Neteru are the forces of Nature.

From the small number of writings which remain to us, it is apparent that these priests were skilled healers who possessed a materials science, much of which is still a mystery to us. There were always two parts to these sciences -- one was mental/spiritual and the other physical. For example, the preparation of a medicine included the processing of a material accompanied by certain words, spells, incantations or rituals. And in prescribing, the patient was given the medicine with instructions to repeat a spell or prayer. The proper timing of these things was equally important.

In the Egyptian Mysteries, Man was composed of various spiritual and mental components as well as the physical component and each had its proper "medicine."

These Secret Sciences advanced over time and tales of wondrous healing oils, life-giving potions, and imitations of gold and precious stones have survived even to our day.

When ancient tomb robbers would plunder a pharaoh's tomb, these precious oils were one of the first things to be stolen. They were considered to be as precious as gold and easier to carry and sell. Stolen gold was heavy and had to be melted down before you could sell it.

When Alexander the Great arrived in Egypt around 300 B.C.E., he fell in love with the whole culture, and the Egyptians welcomed him with open arms. This began the so-called Greco-Egyptian or Ptolemaic period of Egyptian history. The Greeks called Egypt *Khem* or *Khemet*. This literally meant "The Black Land" and is in reference to the thick layer of dark fertile soil deposited by the annual flooding of the Nile. Knowledge of Egyptian Secret Sciences made its way into Greece where it was called *Khemia* "The Black Art" and spawned a long line of Greek alchemists.

In Egypt, Alexander initiated a sweeping campaign of construction and restoration, including the city named after him -- Alexandria. The Great Library of Alexandria is legendary. It has been estimated that this library contained nearly a million volumes of the collected writings of the known world. Scholars from everywhere flocked to Alexandria and it became a melting pot of ideas and philosophies. It is here that the Hermetic Philosophy and alchemy congealed as a Path to Spiritual Attainment and its secrets were only revealed to initiates under an oath of silence.

By around 30 B.C.E., the Roman legions had swept the world and the last of the Egyptian Ptolemies had fallen to Roman rule. During this insurgence, a very large part of the Great Library was destroyed by fire. Initially, Rome was tolerant of Egyptian ways. In fact, the worship of Isis spread well into the Roman world with temples in Rome itself. As the early Roman Emperors became converted to Christianity, this level of tolerance dropped off.

In 290 C.E., the Emperor Diocletian feared that the influx of imitation gold produced by the Egyptian Art could disrupt the Roman economy. Fearing also that it would allow someone to gather enough wealth to form an army which could move against Rome, Diocletian passed an edict calling for the destruction of all texts and materials dealing with the manufacture of gold and precious stones. This order was carried out with great severity.

Great masses of information were indiscriminately destroyed as well as what remained of The Great Library. In 325 C.E., Rome officially became Christian and in 391 the Emperor Theodosius made heresy punishable by death and ordered the destruction of pagan temples. In the Roman world, which at the time covered quite a large area, you were either a Christian or you were exiled or killed.

Most of those practicing the Hermetic Philosophy fled the country and migrated east to Arab lands not occupied by Rome. The early Persian Caliphs were much more hospitable to the alchemists and the center of The Art shifted there, although in a much more guarded capacity. It was here that the Arabic prefix *Al* was added to the Greek **Khemia** to give us *Al-Khemia*, later to become *Alchemy*.

Scientific pursuits in early Christian Rome became dormant for centuries.

With the fall of the Roman Empire, the "civilized world" was thrown into chaos. Thus began "The Dark Ages."

Beginning with the Islamic invasions around 800 C.E., knowledge of alchemy spread into Western Europe, largely through the works of Ibn Sinna (also known as Avicenna.) He formulated a medical system that was popular for several centuries. Another was Abu Musa Jabir ibn Hayaan. Jabir had a very cryptic style of writing, designed to conceal alchemical secrets. It is from his name that we derive our word for *Gibberish*. They collected many of the ancient Egyptian and Greek alchemical works and translated them into Arabic, which were later translated into Latin in Europe.

In Medieval Europe, alchemy became very fashionable. By now, kings and rulers everywhere had heard of the wonders possible through alchemy, especially the turning of lead into gold. Alchemy, as a means to making gold, became a popular pursuit by the rich and the poor. There were also a great number of cons and scams perpetrated by those who pretended to know the secrets of the alchemists. Many unsuspecting people lost their life savings in hopes of finding the way to inexhaustible wealth.

Alchemy began to acquire a bad reputation as a fraud because of this, and people began to distrust the whole matter without really knowing anything about the true alchemical art.Then, around 1310, Pope John XXII issued a decree prohibiting the practice of alchemy, and gold-making in particular, with heavy fines against those who traded in alchemical gold.

In 1404, King Henry IV of England issued an "Act" declaring gold-making a crime against the Crown. By the fifteenth century, the invention of the printing press made knowledge more available to the public. Texts about alchemy became very popular and began to multiply.

Paracelsus (born Phillipus Theophrastus Bombast von Hohenheim in Switzerland 1493) revolutionized the Alchemical Art and is considered to be one of the fathers of modern chemistry and pharmaceutical medicine. A respected physician and university lecturer, Paracelsus was also skilled in all of the arts of the Hermetic Philosophy. Paracelsus repeatedly demonstrated the power and effectiveness of alchemically prepared medicines.

He stressed to his colleagues the importance of looking carefully into alchemy as a source for medicines far beyond what the current pharmaceutical technology could produce. He was constantly at odds with the medical professionals of his day and was looked upon very suspiciously by the Church because of his views and opinions. Because of this some believe Paracelsus was murdered in 1541. However, his ideas and writings did not go unnoticed. In a strange twist of irony, these helped lead to the end of the Age of Alchemy and the beginnings of chemistry as we know it today.

The writings of Paracelsus shifted the view on alchemy from the pursuit of gold into which it had fallen, back toward its original intent -- medicines for the body and soul leading one to perfect health, wholeness, and initiation into Nature's mysteries. Paracelsus recognized man's physical and occult constitution according to Hermetic Principles.

By the seventeenth century, there was a growing religious freedom which sparked a wave of interest in all things Mystical. Alchemical texts became still more widely available, and scholars openly identified themselves as Rosicrucians, Adepts or Alchemists. The spiritual aspects of alchemy appealed to many, apart from any practical works.

Robert Boyle (another "Father of Modern Chemistry") and Isaac Newton studied alchemy during this time. Newton was fully involved and produced volumes of work. In fact, he considered himself to be more of an alchemist than a physicist or mathematician. His notes indicate that he believed he was very close to success in the alchemical art of metallic transmutation.

Boyle was also an ardent student trying to clarify many alchemical concepts which were becoming obscured even in his day. He was a meticulous experimenter and realized the difference between *Philosophical* and *Unphilosophical* workings upon materials.

In his very influential book, *The Sceptical Chymist*, Boyle called into question the number and nature of the elements and called for a more organized terminology. His alchemical insights have been largely misinterpreted to be a debunking of vitalistic alchemy in favor of a more rigorous concentration on the physical facts. It was the beginning of a more mechanical world-view, which would last into the twentieth century.

Around 1660, King Charles II signed the first Charter of the Royal Society and the study of chemistry soon became an officially recognized science.

America also had its alchemists, including several state Governors. There were groups in Pennsylvania who brought with them many of the early German alchemical writings (which were quite extensive.)

By the 1800s, the practice of Alchemy had largely disappeared in the outer world in favor of its still young offshoot -- chemistry. Alchemy survived underground in various "Secret Societies" which became popular, especially towards the end of the nineteenth century.

In the early 1900s, H. Spencer Lewis received a charter from some of these European contacts to form the Ancient Mystical Order of the Rosae Crucis, better known as AMORC. Among other things, they taught laboratory alchemy as it was handed down by earlier Rosicrucian sources.

In the early 1940s, one student of these classes was Albert Reidel. Frater Albertus went on to teach these classes himself and then later split off on his own to establish the Paracelsus Research Society in 1960, which became accredited as Paracelsus College in the early 80s.

With the passing of Frater Albertus in 1984, there seemed to be a void in alchemical teachings and a lack of a central point where students could exchange information. By the early nineties, through the efforts of several PRS students, contact with a French group was made and the Philosophers of Nature (PON) was formulated to fill the void with fresh ideas and to carry on research in alchemy. The PON closed in the late nineties. Now we have the Internet -- the new "Library of Alexandria." As we shall see, chemistry, left to grow unfettered, has nearly come full circle to rediscover the Hermetic Philosophy.

CHAPTER TWO

Theory of Alchemy

The First Law of Hermetics – All is from One

Perhaps the most concise exposition of alchemical theory, acknowledged by adepts from all ages, is the famous "Emerald Tablet of Hermes Trismegistus." Legend has it that this tablet predates the Biblical flood and was inscribed by Thoth himself on a large plate of alchemically produced emerald:

VERBA SECRETORUM HERMETIS

It is true, certain, and without falsehood, that whatever is below is like that which is above; and that which is above is like that which is below: to accomplish the one wonderful work. As all things are derived from the One Only Thing, by the will and by the word of the One Only One who created it in His Mind, so all things owe their existence to this Unity by the order of Nature, and can be improved by Adaptation to that Mind.

Its Father is the Sun; its Mother is the Moon; the Wind carries it in its womb; and its nurse is the Earth. This Thing is the Father of all perfect things in the world. Its power is most perfect when it has again been changed into Earth. Separate the Earth from the Fire, the subtle from the gross, but carefully and with great judgment and skill.

It ascends from earth to heaven, and descends again, new born, to the earth, taking unto itself thereby the power of the Above and the Below. Thus the splendor of the whole world will be thine, and all darkness shall flee from thee.

This is the strongest of all powers, the Force of all forces, for it overcometh all subtle things and can penetrate all that is solid. For thus was the world created, and rare combinations, and wonders of many kinds are wrought.

Hence I am called HERMES TRISMEGISTUS, having mastered the three parts of the wisdom of the whole world. What I have to say about the masterpiece of the alchemical art, the Solar Work, is now ended.

The alchemists always admonish their students, "Know the theory first before attempting the praxis." They say, "You must walk in the Book of Nature to understand our Art."

"The alchemical concept of life and matter lies at the opposite pole of that of the current scientific community. Science is trying to find out how matter created life. Alchemy states that life created matter.

Alchemy affirms that at the origin, there is consciousness. Consciousness is the need to Be of the Absolute.

In order to satisfy this need, consciousness created life, and in order to evolve, life created matter."

-- Jean Dubuis (PON Seminars 1992)

Alchemy is an exploration of the involution of the Absolute into matter and its subsequent evolution back to the source, depicted as the Ouroborus or serpent eating its own tail. There's a very old saying, "The All is mind. The universe is Mental."

The All or The One is, that which is the Fundamental Truth, the Substantial reality, (i.e., standing under and supporting Reality.) This All is beyond comprehending or the ability to truly name it, so we use a symbol and call it -- The All, the Absolute, the Divine, Spirit, the Force, The One Only One. Whatever you choose, it is just a symbol so we can talk about it. This is perhaps best described as Infinite Living Mind.

"Only by mental creation, can the All manifest the universe and still remain the All. For if a substance was used or acted upon, it would be separate and the All would not be All."

--The Kybalion

What we call "matter" is only that portion of the All we apprehend through our senses. It is only a label we use to designate the manifestation of the All within the range of our limited sensory apparatus. All things are connected but separated only by their rates of vibration.

Each one of us is a unique and complex waveform, though we also share many of the same "harmonics." Like fingerprints, we are unique but all related. Modern science takes advantage of this fact in order to identify materials by their vibratory nature in the form of spectral resonances in visible light, infrared, microwaves, etc. Einstein once said, "Everything is energy, beyond that is divine."

19

REAL ALCHEMY

We live in a vast ocean of energy and everything seen and unseen is a part of it. The alchemists called this energy the Celestial Fire, Prima Materia, the First Matter, Chaos, and many others. Everything around us, though it seems separate and different from ourselves is One only One. All is from One is the First Law of Hermetics.

The Second Law of Hermetics -- Polarity

The One reflecting on itself creates the first movement towards polarity -- the division of the One into a most subtle spiritualized energy and dense material energy; the One divided into Spirit and Matter. Today we might call this energy and matter, which are the same.

The Second Law of Hermetics is the law of Polarity.

One of the earliest observations of Nature was that everything has its opposite -- day/night, male/female, hot/cold, wet/dry. The One divides into active and passive modes, with the active energy constituting the energies of life, and the passive one the energy of matter. Consider the image of a sine wave -- two opposite energies but One wave.

The Golden Chain of Homer, a book written about 1730 and highly esteemed by several generations of alchemists, called the active energy "Celestial Niter" and the passive energy "Celestial Salt." We call these "The Volatile" and "The Fixed." These two modes of the One express an inherent polarity as well.

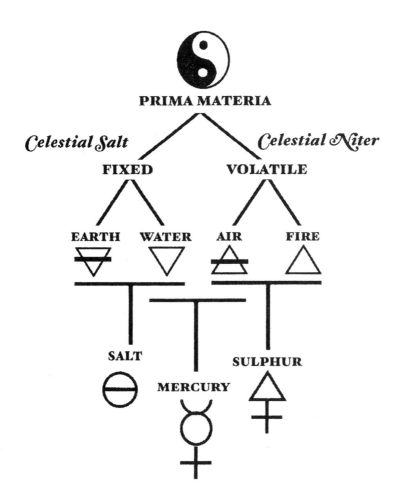

REAL ALCHEMY

The Four Elements

The energy of Life (Niter) operates through the Elements of Fire and Air. Both are active in nature but Fire is the more active of the two. These are the volatile energies. The energy of Matter (Salt) operates through the Elements of Water and Earth. These are the fixed energies -- Water being the more active of the two.

These "Elements" have nothing to do with the material bodies of the same name. They are in fact, energetic states, each with their own unique characteristics. As early as 500 B.C.E., the ancients called these *The Four Elements* and recognized them as the essential qualities by which Nature operates and is formed.

The Element of Fire relates to the qualities of radiance, expansion, warmth, and light -- anciently known as the hot and dry properties. On the psychological level, fire relates to the Superconscious Mind.

The Element of Air is penetrating, diffuse, moveable -- the wet and hot properties. Psychologically, air represents the Selfconscious Mind.

The Element of Water relates to coolness, contraction, mutability or change -- the properties of wet and cold. Water is the perfect representative of the Subconscious Mind.

The Element of Earth relates to the qualities of stability, rest, inertia, strength, and solidity -- the dry and cold properties. In the human economy, this is the physical body.

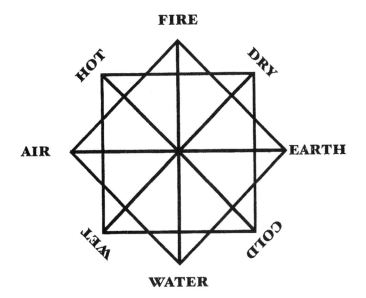

Aristotle's Elements

Modern science agrees that there are "Four Fundamental Forces" governing the activity of everything in our universe and though they call them by the names, "Strong Nuclear Force, Weak Nuclear Force, Electromagnetic Force and Gravitational Force," they are related to the ancient Elemental qualities of Fire, Water, Air and Earth respectively.

These elemental qualities and their mixtures form the vehicles through which the alchemical "Three Essentials" operate. They are the clothing which we interpret as our physical reality.

23

The Three Essentials

The *Three Essentials* are the alchemical principles of Sulfur, Mercury, and Salt. Again these terms are not the common materials we associate with these words, such as table salt or the mercury in your thermometer. They describe subtle philosophical principles active in Nature.

Alchemical Salt, or the **Body** of a thing, provides the matrix wherein the Sulfur and Mercury can act. It is a passive medium, the Virgin Earth, subject to the fixed energies of Water and Earth. The Salt is influenced by psychic and instinctual forces of the subconscious as well as the conditions affecting the various states of matter.

The Alchemical Sulfur, or **Soul** of a thing, conducts the volatile principles of Fire and Air expressing consciousness, intellect, and the "True Will" or personal fire.

Alchemical Mercury, or the **Spirit** of a thing, is the vital force or life force, and predominates in the elements of Air and Water, reflecting intellectual, instinctual and psychic energies. It forms the link or bridge, between the higher forces of Sulfur and the lower body of matter, the Salt. In mythology, Mercury is the messenger between the world of the Gods and the world of mortals -- the physical world.

The energies of Celestial Niter are often equated with the force of *Kundalini*, our internal spiritual force according to Indian philosophy. In alchemy, this is referred to as the *Secret Fire in Man*. The energies of Celestial Salt are equated with the force of *Prana*, or Vital Energy carried by the air we breathe and food we eat. Prana is the primary energy distributed throughout the cosmos, said to maintain physical life and existence. It acts at the instinctual and unconscious levels as well as being influenced by cosmic cycles and other natural phenomena.

The function of the Kundalini / Niter is to increase awareness of our True Self and True Will by lifting our consciousness and opening us to wider vistas of awareness. At the lowest level of functioning, this is the self-centered ego, at its highest, we become aware of our Divine nature.

24

The effects of awakening this Secret Fire within constitute a true awakening into nature's mysteries with attendant changes in our perception of how Nature operates. This is a direct experience of liberating interior knowledge. The physical body is also changed and improved in functioning, establishing a new center of balance on spiritual and physical levels.

The alchemical process seeks to fan this fire... "carefully, with great judgment and skill." In laboratory alchemy, the Three Essentials of Body, Soul, and Spirit are most important because they provide us a means of manipulating the elements. Many alchemists indicate that the Primal Elements are too subtle even for the most skilled artist and that only Nature can work at that level. The Three Essentials are the fruit of the Elements, which Man can manipulate even at the physical level. As the Polish alchemist Michael Sendivogius wrote in his "New Chemical Light" about 1600:

> "The three principles of things are produced out of the four elements in the following manner: Nature, whose power is in her obedience to the Will of God, ordained from the very beginning, that the four elements should incessantly act on one another, so, in obedience to her behest, the fire began to act on air, and produced Sulfur; air acted on water and produced Mercury; water, by its action on earth, produced Salt.
>
> Earth alone, having nothing to act upon, did not produce anything, but became the nurse, or womb, of these three principles."

In summary then:

The **Salt** represents the **Body**, or vehicle, which allows expression of the other two essentials. It is a principle of fixity, consolidation, and focus -- The Material Basis, or matrix.

The **Sulfur**, represents the **Soul**, the Consciousness. It is a fiery principle, brightness. The Spiritualized Male aspect of the One. Kundalini. The character of a thing. The True Colors. The Intelligence. The Divine Spark.

The **Mercury**, represents the **Spirit** -- the Vital Life Force, the Animating Spirit, Chi, Prana. It is a Subtle, spiritualized Feminine aspect of the One. Pure Energy. It bridges the Air and Water Elements, the Spiritual World and the Material World, the Volatile and the Fixed.

It is the Sulfur (the Consciousness) which directs the Life Force through the body. Directing more of the Life Force through more refined bodies or vehicles is the course of Nature and Evolution. Alchemical work strives to create and fortify an incorruptible spiritual body of which the physical body is a reflection.

The Three Kingdoms -- Vegetable, Animal, Mineral

To the alchemist, everything is alive and consists of a Body, Soul and Spirit or Salt, Sulfur and Mercury. This is true in the Vegetable Kingdom, the Animal Kingdom and the Mineral Kingdom. That the plant world and the animal world are filled with living beings is obvious to all.

The mineral world is generally looked upon as non-living because we only understand carbon based life, but to the alchemist the mineral world is also teaming with life and consciousness just as much as the other two kingdoms. The processes of alchemy reach into each of the three kingdoms in order to bring its subjects to a higher degree of perfection.

In alchemy, all things are evolving but considered to be exposed to a wave of energies becoming involved in matter as well, and thus subject to hindrances and impurities from matter not ready or mature enough to evolve beyond a certain level (corruptible matter). As a result the energies of life are weakened and the energies of matter predominate when it is the energies of life which should predominate.

The alchemist believed that by understanding Nature's laws and applying them with Art, that it is possible to remove hindrances to the evolutionary wave so that the energies of life can predominate and lift the subject toward perfection.

Nature is the greatest alchemist of all. She has all of time to complete the process of evolution which is constantly unfolding around us like a symphony. The alchemist seeks to assist in this evolution utilizing Nature's own laws and methods. In the Laboratory, the alchemist can demonstrate Nature's laws at work and can speed the processes up.

Sacred Cycles

Early observations of Nature revealed that she moves in cycles, that there is a rhythm to everything. Vibration is a periodic event, circular in nature. Everything we see, everything we know of is vibration and because of this, there are certain harmonies established between things.

From early times people have observed the stars in order to understand the rhythm of Nature. If one intends to help the process of evolution, one has to keep within Nature's laws. You would not go out and plant lettuce in the snow. So it is in the Laboratory, where the alchemist would await a specific time to carry out an operation in order to capture the momentum of subtle forces.

There are many such connections between gardening and alchemical works.

CHAPTER THREE

Astrology and Alchemy

As Above So Below

Astrology is intimately connected with the Hermetic Philosophy and supplies much of the guidance for practical applications of the Alchemist's Art.

The forces of nature have their reflection at all levels of reality -- the Salt, Sulfur and Mercury.

Man is a microcosm inseparable from his macrocosmic environment.

The Sun has always been considered the source of all life and light in our system. The Sun radiates out; the planets absorb what they need then radiate the excess.

This forms the complex interplay of subtle energies that reach our planet and form the basis for astrological studies. The stars also exert their energies and enter into this constant interplay. Advances in Radio Astronomy have shown that we are constantly receiving energy "fingerprints" from many stars as well as the planets.

In practice, all things are considered to be the product of their natural cycles. For example, medicinal plants are harvested at the correct time in relation to the plant part required.

When the plant is operated on in the laboratory, each stage should be done at an optimal astrological configuration harmonious to that operation. It has been said that without knowledge of astrological tools and methods, the production of a true alchemical medicine is not possible.

Each illness appears like a vibratory disharmony or dissonance to our particular waveform or field. Using a system of correspondences, alchemical medicine seeks to restore the harmony of our true selves.

From ancient traditions to modern scientific studies, we know that medicinal herbs have physiological effects on specific organ systems. Herbs, like the organs they affect, are considered to fall under the influence of a particular planet or sign of the zodiac on the basis of an affinity.

Each planetary sphere has a unique energetic expression and signature qualities associated with it, such as color, musical tones, parts of the body, diseases, medical effects, herbs, stones and metals. For example, the planet Venus is said to be the "ruler" of Copper metal and the herb Yarrow, as well as affecting the kidneys in man.

This rulership is a two-way interaction called sympathy, and refers to the planetary energies as they affect our world, and things of this world manifesting the different qualities of these planetary energies. Today we might describe this "sympathy" as resonance. Each thing below then, has a characteristic waveform resonating with planetary energies from above in specific ways.

Within man's occult anatomy, these planetary representatives were often referred to as our "Interior Stars."

In Practical Alchemy, the timing of astrological events is used to assist various aspects of the work on the three levels -- Salt, Sulfur, and Mercury.

In the work with plants, the Moon's disposition is a very important consideration.

The Waxing Moon is good for *Enriching an Essential* element by circulations or distillations. Its magnetic influence draws things up -- volatilizing, exalting and spiritualizing them. The Waning Moon is good for *Separating the Pure from the Impure* whether by distillation, extraction, or calcinations, etc. Just as the dying moonlight, our matter is subjected to the fermentation and putrefaction of death in order to release its essence, thus separating the pure and the impure.

Astrology helps to harness subtle forces, which have an influence on our subject matter. That there are physical forces at play has been demonstrated through studies such as crystallization experiments, and capillary dynamics; but there is also a subtle, spiritual aspect we seek to capture as well. Our material subject is the magnet which gathers the energy and holds it.

The Importance of the Birth Chart

Our personal natal horoscope provides us with a powerful tool for understanding our own energy signature and how it is affected by other energy forms including matter. A detailed examination of the birth chart takes time, but reveals one's essence.

The first concepts to examine in order to use this system are the individual planets and zodiacal signs, their energies, and rulerships. By developing an understanding of these sympathies and their interactions with each other, we can work to rectify the energetic imbalances that can lead to illness, and also work to strengthen specific energies within ourselves for physical or spiritual improvement.

Each individual at birth is considered to be of a particular zodiac type in that their energetic imprint predisposes them to a particular temperament and also a predisposition to an organ weakness which is peculiar to that sign of the zodiac.

There are a few approaches to working with planetary energies for healing. The most simple is to use the individual planetary energies to support organs, systems, or functions of the body, or use them to oppose disorders, all according to planetary rulership.

Another technique for using the planetary system of healing involves a more in-depth study of the birth chart and of the whole self, rather than just the treatment of passing symptoms and illnesses. It offers much deeper and longer-lasting balance and wellness. In this approach, the birth information of the individual is examined, and planetary affinities are determined.

31

The concept behind this is that at the time of birth, the planetary energies are locked up in physical material and have a determined reflection, stamping their
influences and energies at each level of being. The rulership of the various houses in the birth chart reveals all types of personal qualities, such as strengths, weaknesses, disease and health tendencies, and affinities for certain methods of treatment.

The planetary energies can also be deliberately introduced in order to produce certain effects in the body, mind, or spiritual level of a person. Each planetary influence can be experienced and worked with in turn to create physical and spiritual balance.

In alchemical works, the pattern of life/death/rebirth is often repeated upon the subject in various forms. For example, during distillation, our liquid passes into an invisible state then condenses and manifests in an improved form. The alchemists viewed this as analogous to death, a visit to the spiritual world then rebirth in the physical. Similarly during recrystallization, our matter is dissolved into a medium and becomes clear, then made to reappear as an improved form. In astrology, the birth chart shows the imprint of the cosmos on the individual at birth. So too during those periods of rebirth of our matter there is the imprint of the heavens. By repeatedly reinforcing a particular planetary power during these multiple rebirths, our subject becomes polarized to that force.

CHAPTER FOUR

Introduction to Laboratory Alchemy

"It is therefore necessary that theory is accompanied by practice, the one being the consequence of the other. Only laboratory practice gives mastership, for what is practice if not controlled by theory. The rigor of the former corrects the vagaries of the latter. The disciple must exert himself to realize all his concepts."

-- Magaphon's Commentary on "Mutus Liber"

In Practical Alchemy, there is only the One Thing and all that we perceive is an adaptation of that One. The One takes on the "Clothing" of the Four Elements to bring forth the Three Essentials of Sulfur, Mercury, and Salt. It is the Work of the alchemist to separate, purify and recombine these basic principles until they are in perfect proportion and harmony with each other.

Alchemy is all about bringing things to a greater state of perfection.

"Everything which is generated of its elements is divided into three, namely into Salt, Sulfur, and Mercury. Learn the form which is peculiar to these three. One is liquor, and this is the form of Mercury; one is oiliness which is the form of Sulfur; one is alkali, and this is from Salt."

--Paracelsus

Spagyrics

The three philosophical essentials are mirrored even to the physical level, and manifested through particular forms which are harmonious to their nature. The Practical Alchemist seeks to physically separate these three essentials from a substance, purify them, and recombine them -- a process termed *Spagyrics* by Paracelsus. The word *Spagyric* (pronounced "spa jeer ik") is derived from the Greek words meaning "to separate and reunite."

The general process used in Spagyrics consists of three main steps:

1. Separation (of the Three Essentials)
2. Purification
3. Cohobation (or recombining)

Learning to *spagyrically* prepare herbs is a typical starting point for laboratory alchemy. It provides experiences which develop skill and understanding of the Art and Science involved, and can provide you with some very powerful remedies along the way.

These first experiments with plants lead the way to the "Lesser Circulation" or Plant Stone (which is very similar to the "Greater Circulation" which produces the Philosopher's Stone.)

Before we talk about the easy method, I want to describe the process in another more detailed fashion because I think it more clearly illustrates the separation of the Three Essentials. Let us say that we have selected the Sun-ruled herb Rosemary to work upon.

With an eye to the Sun and Moon's disposition, we gather some fresh Rosemary, chop it finely and place it into a flask with a little water to make paste. We let it stand awhile to loosen up, then steam is injected into the herb paste and the hot vapors arising are captured in a cooling condenser. This distillate contains water from the steam and floating on the water will form a layer of oil -- the essential oil of Rosemary.

34

This oil we collect. It is the first of the Three Essentials and represents what the alchemists called the *Alchemical Sulfur* of the plant. The oil is a material analog or vehicle for the subtle principle of Sulfur, the Soul or character of the plant.

Our Rosemary remains in the flask as a watery mush and we allow this to ferment. In fermentation, the plant "dies" and "gives up the ghost" -- that is to say, the life force departs into the watery medium. After fermentation we can distill from this mush a volatile liquid which the ancients called the *Alchemical Mercury*. This volatile liquid, which is mainly alcohol, carries the Spirit of the plant -- the life force. Today we still buy "spirits" at the liquor store and this is where the term comes from.

Remember, these physical materials are a reflection of the spiritual forces in Nature. The alcohol contains the life force as its body in this realm. The alcohol is not the spirit but merely a vehicle of spirit in the plant world, a focal point.

We now have *separation* of the Three Essentials, the oil or Sulfur, the Mercury as alcohol, and the Salt, which still lies hidden in the extracted Rosemary residue.

The next step of the process is the *purification* of our separated essentials. The Mercury and Sulfur are redistilled a number of times until they are highly refined in the physical sense, but also exalted in the spiritual sense.

To obtain the Salt, the extracted plant material is dried and then incinerated to an ash. This purges the accumulated impurities and structural components, which protected the plant in its growing environment. They have served their purpose but are no longer necessary. The light gray to white ash we obtain is dissolved in water, filtered and the liquid is then evaporated leaving a purified white crystalline salt. This represents the *Alchemical Salt*, the true body of the plant. With the separation and purification of our three essentials complete, we move on to the final step of the Spagyric process, that of *cohobation*.

In a sort of resurrection, the finely powdered Salt is saturated with its Sulfur and awakened into activity by addition of its life force, the Mercury. After a period of digestion, our "Elixir" is complete. The alchemists considered such preparations to be exalted and evolved living medicines able to express the plant's true healing potentials not only on the body but at the level of the soul and spirit as well.

> "When now the Spiritus and Corpus come together and are united after their preparation, one can do wonderful things with them, since they have then a hundred times more power than they had previously, for after the Conjunctio of the Souls and Body there exists a Glorified Corpus and a Great Elixir. With it one performs miracles."
>
> -- Isaac Holland (circa 1480)

The Easy Method

OK, now for the easy method. Everyone can do this and you probably have most of the materials at home.

The Mercury **within a kingdom is universal.** The life force that animates me is the same as that within each of you. The spirit we distill from one plant is largely the same as we would obtain from distilling any other fermented plant. That being the case we can easily obtain our first Essential from the local liquor store. (They sell spirits.)

Ideally, we would buy Everclear, which is 95% alcohol (but this depends on which State you live in.) 100 proof vodka is usually available. This is 50% alcohol and is a satisfactory medium for this beginning operation, but we can use any strong alcohol for this first operation provided that <u>Only Potable Alcohol</u> is used. Do not use De-Natured Alcohol or Methanol.

The Mercury of each kingdom has an affinity for the Sulfur of that kingdom.

So to begin, take a plant you wish to work with, and grind it to a fine powder. Place the powder into a jar (a canning jar works well) then pour your alcohol over the powder to cover it by one or two finger widths. Place a piece of plastic wrap over the top and screw the lid on tightly. (The plastic wrap prevents contact with the metal top.)

Place the sealed jar into a warm place out of direct light. The top of a water heater is a good spot. Let this stand for about two weeks and remember to shake it well every day. After the two weeks are up you will see that the alcohol has become deeply colored. We want to collect this extract and a good way to do it is to pour the entire contents into an old nylon stocking placed into a second jar. Wearing rubber gloves, squeeze the nylon to obtain as much of the liquid as possible, then seal the jar and let it stand. This liquid extract contains the combined Mercury and Sulfur of the plant.

Take the extracted plant residue and place it into a fire-resistant dish outside. Touch a match to the herb and let it burn down to an ash. Grind the ash very fine and return it to the dish. Then place it over a gas burner or in the oven under broil to make it as light gray to white as possible. This ash contains the Salt principle of the plant.

Quickly grind the ash while still warm, then add it to the extract of the plant you collected earlier. Again seal the jar and let it stand in a warm place for at least a week. Shake the jar daily very well.

At the end of the week, filter the liquid through a coffee filter and let it stand in a clean glass container for about forty-eight hours to see if any more insolubles settle out. Decant the clarified extract into dropper bottles for use. This is now a simple Spagyric elixir containing the three essentials of the plant in an exalted form and able to express the plant's truest and most powerful healing potentials on the various levels of our constitution.

Remember that in each of these operations, if we can work with conscious intent and create a sacred space to work from, the more effective the end result will be. We also want to keep within astrological timings favorable to the plant as much as we are able.

If one is skilled in astrology, one can elect a powerful time to work the various operations. Perhaps the easiest thing to do here in these beginning experiments is to take note of the waxing / waning Moon as we mentioned earlier and also work on the day whose planet rules the herb we operate on (preferably within the hour following sunrise.)

Creating the Seven Basics

Our suggestion here is that you create what are known as the "Seven Basics." By utilizing the Spagyric methods just described, one can create Seven Elixirs -- one for each day of the week.

Your Sun herb elixir is taken on Sunday, a Moon herb elixir on Monday, and so on. A few drops in a small amount of water or wine is a good way to start. This will begin to gently harmonize each system of the body and start the process of rebalancing and transformation at all levels. See the Appendix for information on herbs and their ruling planets.

You really are what you eat. By using these Seven Basics over time, their refined and spiritualized matter become part of you and in turn you become more refined and spiritualized.

It is said that the attitude of the artist, more than the process itself, is what makes alchemy "The Divine Art." This attitude and energy becomes transferred to the matter being acted upon and affects the outcome of the operation. The energy is released again within us from the Elixir in a more noble state.

You are the lead which is transmuted into pure gold. As with any new skill, we start with simple things and progress to more complex operations as our skill and experience lead us. We have to make a start somewhere, and these simple procedures form the beginnings of a fascinating process of self-transformation.

CHAPTER FIVE

Alchemical Processes

I want to mention something about Spagyrics vs. Alchemy vs. Chemistry.

In chemistry, we take certain ingredients and combine them through a process to obtain a certain result. And it is always the same result whether I mix it or you mix it. In alchemy this is not always the case. There is a subtle something, which can influence the end result.

The chemist works with materials which are compounded and purified by processes, which the alchemist would call *Unphilosophical* and the materials so produced are dead bodies only. So what is *Philosophical*? To have your materials be philosophically produced means you must follow the philosophy of alchemy and realize that you are working with the life force and consciousness of your materials as well as the body. Again, the quality of our attention affects the quality of life in our subject just as with a houseplant or pet.

The processes used in laboratory alchemy strive to capture and preserve the operation of subtle essences in a suitable vehicle all the way to their material analogs.

Between 1600 and 1700 there occurred a transition period between alchemy and the new science of chemistry. It is during this time period that we can find some of the most clearly written descriptions of processes used in alchemy.

Apothecaries of the time were acquainted with the processes and used them to compound certain medicines. This branch of the pharmacy at that time came to be known as Spagyrics and related mostly to the preparation of plants. Spagyric preparations became widely popular but due largely to the long processing times and labor, they slowly faded into obscurity at the hands of faster, cheaper substitutes born of a developing chemical industry.

Some writers say Spagyrics is the work on plants and alchemy is the work on metals. In truth, alchemy is a universal process working at all levels. Whereas the Spagyric process is fundamental to both, alchemy in addition seeks to promote the matter's evolution. In a practical sense, Spagyrics leads to powerful medicines for the body. Anyone who follows the methods can produce Spagyric medicines. There is no strong dependence on the operator's state of mind.

Alchemy aims to produce medicines for the soul and spirit levels of being, as well as the body, and the operator is strongly linked to the material operated upon. The proper state of mind is essential for success. For example, once you have purified your essentials to a certain degree, they become very susceptible to mental impressions by those around them -- good or bad. This is another reason for the secrecy surrounding alchemical works. Very often, only the artist is allowed to see or handle materials at certain points. These processes and materials can lead to deep insight or contact with alternate realms of consciousness, thus bringing direct knowledge to the alchemist. This is a type of knowing that can not be written because words are too limiting. It is the marriage of intellect and intuition or the Sun and the Moon, as the alchemists would say.

Alchemy is more than just something you do in a laboratory. It is a spiritual path leading one to enlightenment -- to evolving. It can be thought of as a psycho-physiological transformation directed by human self-consciousness.

The Great Work, or *Magnum Opus* of alchemy, leads to the spiritual and physical regeneration of the alchemist himself.

The Philosophers agree that the process consists of stages, which are repeated over and over again on the matter until perfection is obtained. These stages or Operations, represent the active principles at work in nature whether we are speaking of the work on plants, metals or on our own body and psyche. The alchemical work is not just a "spring cleaning" or "detox session" from which we fall back into the same routine. Instead it is a true and lasting purification.

That portion of The Great Work which has to do with the transmutation of the alchemist himself is a process whereby the vibratory activity of our "interior stars" is so modified that the lower rates of vibration are transmuted and sublimated, or lifted up.

This transmutation of the subtle force working through the interior stars has a triple consequence. It leads to spiritual illumination. It presents the alchemist with radiant health, due to the perfect combination and coordination of chemical and electrical energies, which maintain the form and functioning of the human body. And finally, this process opens the activity of powers which are normally dormant in most human beings. Paracelsus said, "You will transmute nothing if you have not first transmuted yourself."

Man himself is the primary subject of the Hermetic Art. It is useless to try to make the Philosopher's Stone outside oneself before one has approached the first part of the operation, which slowly transforms the operator himself into the Living Stone. Only then will the Alchemist possess the necessary skill and understanding of subtle forces to complete the work of making an actual substance with the power to transmute other bodies.

The study of Astrology and practical Qabalah provide us with tools for establishing relationships between seemingly unrelated concepts and materials as well as a technology for the raising of spiritual energy, the Secret Fire in Man. These are essential parts of the alchemist's discipline. Trying to separate out the physical actions of the alchemist in the laboratory from these interior connections, bridging the spiritual and physical realms, reduces it to common chemistry.

REAL ALCHEMY

Ora Et Labora

The alchemical dictum "Ora Et Labora" (pray and work) was the ancient guideline for practice. Our word "laboratory" comes from it. The lab is a temple and oratory wherein we labor.

The laboratory work provides us with some powerful tools for accomplishing this Great Work. The creation of our tinctures and elixirs is a first step in correcting the imbalances in our own Sulfur, Mercury, and Salt. But there are many improvements that can be made to augment their power and effectiveness. Some are simple; others require much more time and effort.

Each process teaches and provides insight into Nature's operations. Before we can approach this subject however, we need to understand something of the methodology of laboratory alchemy.

Many people have the impression that to even begin alchemical work, one must have all manner of expensive chemical apparatus at one's disposal. Not true. You can begin your own alchemical laboratory with common household items just as we did in preparing the "Seven Basics." As one continues the Work, one finds that the materials one needs have a way of showing up when they are needed.

In the laboratory, fire is our main tool for transformation. Alchemy has been called the **Work of Vulcan** (blacksmith of the gods) and the old masters called themselves **Fire Philosophers**. The Sages agree that control of the fire is the key to success in alchemical works.

Not very long ago, there were no thermostatic controls like we have today, and not much further back, there were no thermometers. Yet the alchemists were able to perform delicate distillations as well as prolonged searing heats of materials using coal and charcoal furnaces. Anyone who has ever stoked a woodstove or campfire (or even a barbeque) must appreciate the dedication and diligence required to keep a crucible at red heat for a month or even longer using a coal furnace.

The Four Degrees of Fire

There are many grades of fire mentioned in alchemical texts. Some are physical, some are subtle representatives of spiritual principles. Most often mentioned are Celestial Fire, Central Fire, Secret Fire, and Elemental or Common Fire. We will be developing a deeper understanding of these various fires as we go. For now, let us examine the lowest grade of fire, that which we are most familiar with -- common fire.

At the practical level, the ancients used Common Fire in a system of graded heats often called the Four Degrees of Fire.

The first degree of fire is the ***Balneum Marie*** or Bath of Mary. Some believe this was developed by a female Jewish adept named Mary (the prophetess) around 500 C.E. (Others say it is not derived from a woman's name, but from the word "mare" and refers to the ocean -- like marine.)

This is basically a double boiler. The container of matter to be heated is immersed in another container of water, which is heated by the furnace. In this way the subject matter can never get hotter than 100°C and thus can not scorch the delicate components. Alcohol is rectified in a water bath, as an example.

The second degree of fire is ***Balneum Cinerus*** or ash bath. This is where the matter is placed in the ash pit and heated still hotter. The ashes have a certain insulating quality that allows for a heat which is above that of boiling water but still evenly distributed around the vessel.

The third degree of heat is called the ***Balneum Arena*** or sand bath. It is set up like the water bath but it is able to maintain a higher heat than the water or ashes. Many oils and substances with boiling points higher than water can be heated and distilled with the sand bath. It provides an even heating of the matter and avoids hot spots from developing. In fairly high heats, the sand bath also lends support for the vessel which might otherwise become deformed from the heat.

The fourth degree is ***Balneum Ignis*** or bathed in flame. This is the hottest you can make it in your furnace with a naked flame. This heat is used for calcinations, fusions, etc.

We have a great advantage today with our electric hot plates or gas heating that can be regulated easily for long periods. In general, start off with the lowest temperature possible to accomplish the operation and try to avoid hot spots from uneven heating. One can always increase the heat as needed.

The Alchemical Operations

We mentioned earlier that the operations of alchemy are representative of nature's operative principles active at all levels of reality. The Sages often point out that knowledge of the occult operations of the elements is another essential key to success. In order to understand where and why a particular operation is applied to our matter in the laboratory, we will be examining alchemical concepts of the elements as we go along.

DISTILLATION

I want to talk about some of the common operations in laboratory alchemy and hopefully allay some of the fears in their performance. Foremost in this is the process of distillation. You have all done this. Maybe you did not recognize it as such. You put a pot on the stove to simmer, then return to check it, lift the lid and liquid streams off. This liquid has distilled from the contents of the pot. You breathe on a cold glass window and it condenses to liquid drops. This is distillation.

The earliest accounts of distillation describe hanging flocks of wool over boiling pots then wringing the distilled liquid from the wool.

> "Now I am come to the arts, and I shall begin from Distillation an invention of later times, a wonderful thing, to be praised beyond the power of man, not that which the vulgar and unskillful man may use. For they do but corrupt and destroy what is good. But that which is done by skillful artists. This admirable art, teaches how to make spirits, and sublime gross bodies,

and how to condense, and make spirits become gross bodies. And to draw forth of plants, minerals, stones and jewels, the strength of them, that are involved and overwhelmed with great bulk, lying hid, as it were, in their chests. And to make them more pure, and thin, and more noble, as not being content with their common condition, and so lift them up as high as heaven."

-- Jean Baptiste Dela Porta 1600

You can go a long way in alchemy by gaining some mastery in the art of distillation. In days passed, many households contained a distillery for making medicines, cordials, and cosmetics.

There are many types of distillation -- simple, fractional, steam, vacuum, solar, etc. In chemistry we use this process to separate liquids from one another, and to purify liquids. In alchemy, we additionally use this process to exalt or evolve our matter (as we mentioned earlier) mirroring the life, death, rebirth cycle between states of matter.

A trip to the thrift store and some ingenuity can provide you with a simple distillation set-up if you do not have the funds or inclination to purchase chemistry glassware or if you want to just try your hand at it before investing in glassware. At the very simplest, a jar containing liquid to be distilled can be placed into a larger jar which is then sealed and placed in a sunny spot. The distillate will form on the walls of the large jar and run down the sides to the bottom where it is collected. It may not be terribly efficient or suitable for all distillations, but it is easily available for anyone to experiment. There are many illustrations in old texts depicting this type of solar distillation.

In herbal alchemy, most common uses of distillation are in the preparation of the Sulfur and Mercury. Earlier we described the steam distillation of the essential oils from a plant. Live steam is injected into a plant / water mush and the essential oils are carried over with the steam to form a layer on top of the distilled water. We can also simply distill the plant / water mush and collect the oil as it forms a layer at the top of the

45

distillate. The collected oil can be mixed with water and distilled again to bring it to a higher state of purity.

The distillation of alcohol is perhaps the most frequent operation in herbal alchemy and this distillation is repeated anywhere from six to twelve times in order to make it pure enough. This process is called *Rectification*. However we cannot produce 100% alcohol by simple distillation no matter how often you repeat the process. The best we can do is about 95% unless we use some new tricks. Most often a drying agent is used such as potassium carbonate or calcium oxide (quicklime.) These materials are not soluble in alcohol but have a voracious affinity for water, which they absorb from the alcohol. In many instances, the distillations are repeated not so much to increase the purity but to elevate or spiritualize the matter.

DIGESTION

This is one of the most common operations of practical alchemy and is simply allowing a material to incubate at a constant temperature for some period of time. The time period will vary depending on what is needed to occur and the temperature may need to be slowly increased over a lengthy course of digestion, but the idea is to provide a heated environment for the matter to react within or to slowly mature like hatching an egg. The whole of the Art is a controlled digestion.

You can construct a simple chamber for digestion by placing a lightbulb inside a large plastic ice chest of the type used for camping. Simply by changing the wattage of the lamp you can control the temperature to the required degree. A simple indoor/outdoor thermometer is useful for monitoring temperature, which for herbal work ranges from about 90 to 104 degrees F. Many operators prefer to wrap vessels with aluminum foil to protect them from the bright light.

EXTRACTION

Extraction refers to methods for separating the pure from the impure. As with all of these basic operations, there are many ways to accomplish the end.

In general, extraction methods use an extraction medium to effect separation. When you brew tea, water is the extraction medium; when you made the seven basics, vodka was the extraction medium. Remember that the Mercury of a kingdom has an affinity for the Sulfur of that kingdom. In herbal extraction we use alcohol, the vehicle for vegetable Mercury, to pull out the Sulfur of the plant. The resulting extract is called a tincture from the Latin "tinctura", that which colors. It contains the Mercury and Sulfur of the plant. The extracted plant residue contains the salt which we obtain by calcination.

There are three methods widely used to effect extraction of a tincture from plants, the first is called Maceration. We used this to make the seven basics.

Pour the extraction media, also called the solvent or menstruum, over the material to be extracted until it stands about two finger widths above the material.

Seal tightly and shake well. Place into a warm spot to digest and remember to shake it daily. After the extraction period, which can be a few hours to over a year in some operations, simply filter the tincture to separate it from the residue.

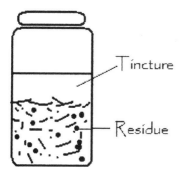

Maceration

The second type of extraction allows us to use a greater heat without loss of the volatile components. This method is called a Reflux Extraction. The matter to be extracted is placed into a flask and covered with the extraction medium. Then a condenser is attached to the top and heat is applied such that condensation occurs no higher than the first 1/3 of the condenser. After several days of this constant heating without liquid loss, the material is allowed to cool then filtered to obtain the extract and solid residue. This method works well for harder materials such as roots, barks and woods.

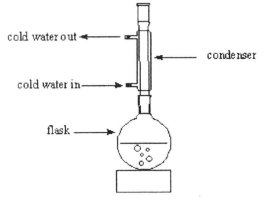

cold water out

condenser

cold water in

flask

The third method of extraction is called Soxhlet Extraction, named after Franz Von Soxhlet a German chemist who invented a special glassware apparatus for extracting fatty substances from materials in 1879. The apparatus has come to be called a Soxhlet Extractor and can be somewhat expensive. In this method, the material to be extracted is placed into a filter paper cup, called a "thimble", and inserted into the extractor body. The extraction medium is placed into the flask at the bottom and heat is applied to it. The solvent vapors rise up a side tube into a condenser where it turns to liquid again and drops into the extractor body and thimble. The extractor body fills with solvent until it reaches the top of the siphon tube whereupon it drains back into the flask. This cycle repeats until extraction is complete and there is no more coloring of solvent in the extractor body. The extract or tincture is recovered from the flask and the extracted residue is recovered from the thimble. Very often several thimbles are filled and extracted with the same solvent to obtain a concentrated tincture.

FERMENTATION

Fermentation is a very important process in alchemy through which the vital essence of a material is released into a new medium from which we can capture it. In herbal alchemy it is always preferable to use the plant's own Mercury instead of that derived from another source such as grain alcohol. Although the Mercury of a kingdom is the same throughout that kingdom, isolating it in this very purified form is difficult. Each type of alcohol carries with it some of the subtle Sulfur of the plant from which it was distilled. In many of the beginning works of herbal alchemy and for general use, an alcohol derived from wine is perfectly suitable; however, for some of the more advanced works, it will be necessary to obtain the alcohol from the particular plant one is working with.

Winemaking is an art unto itself and more than we can detail here. You can explore this in many places online, so we will only touch on a few guidelines for alchemical work. The ideal is to add nothing foreign to the plant, that is, no added yeasts, or sugar, or nutrients other than what the plant itself supplies. The general procedure is to place the fresh or dried plant into a large container that can be sealed. If you are using plant materials that have been steamed to collect the Sulfur, the natural yeasts of the plant are going to be inactive so you will have to add a handful of the plant that did not get steamed. Cover the plant matter with enough water to make it very liquid, say five to ten times the volume of solids and stir it around very well. Now stopper the vessel tightly but leave a small piece of tubing running out of the top and into a small container of water. This is called a fermentation lock. Fermentation is anaerobic, that is, it proceeds without air contact; however, there is release of carbon dioxide gas which can bubble out of the tube without air getting in. Fermentation can take days or weeks to complete so place the vessel into a

49

warm place at about 30 degrees C and watch for the bubbling to stop. When the bubbling and foaming action has stopped, filter the liquid out and seal it for use. You can proceed immediately to distillation in order to obtain the Mercury or let the "wine" age for awhile first.

Remember to save the plant residue for calcination and recovery of the Salt and also save the liquid from which you distilled the Mercury. This liquid is evaporated to a thick honey-like consistency then calcined to obtain the Salt of Sulfur of the plant (more on this when we talk about calcination).

In practice, you may find it necessary to deviate from the ideal and add a small amount of wine yeast and sugar to those plants that seem to refuse to ferment easily.

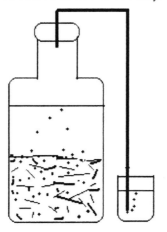

If you find it necessary to add yeast to initiate fermentation, try adding a handful of red grapes which still have the white, powdery coating of natural yeast on the skins, into a cupful of warm water. Shake it around for awhile, then decant the water, which now contains some of the grape yeast, into the plant/water mixture you wish to ferment. This will act as a starter to initiate fermentation.

SUBLIMATION

Sublimation is a term used to denote the rarefaction of a material and though it is often applied to liquid or solid materials in alchemy, it most commonly refers to action on a solid body. There are some solids you will come upon in alchemy which are purified by sublimation. These materials go from the solid state to a vapor without passing through a liquid state and the vapor returns to the solid state upon contact with a cool surface.

Alchemically, the body opens and the finer parts ascend. These are captured by a cool condensing surface in an exalted form. Most notable are many of the ammonia-based salts. Corning Ware casseroles work well for this. Place the matter to be sublimated in a layer on the bottom of one casserole, then cover with a second casserole that is inverted. Gently heat the bottom and the sublimate will collect on the upper surfaces. The final sublimation temperature will depend on the matter you are sublimating and can range from near room temperature to a full red heat.

Sublimation is the reason your ice cubes disappear if left for long periods in the freezer and forms the basis for freeze drying materials.

CIRCULATION

Circulation is a process of continuous distillation used in alchemy to evolve your subject matter. In its simplest form, your subject (say one of the Seven Basics) is placed into a tall bottle like a long wine bottle and gently heated at the bottom while the top is allowed to remain cool. In this way the liquid distills upward, hits the cool upper surface and condenses; then falls back into the bulk of the liquid. It is not unusual to let a substance circulate for a month or longer during which time it passes through many life and death re-birth cycles and is evolved.

This is another easy method of enhancing the effectiveness of your elixirs and of stepping from the realm of simple Spagyric preparation to truly alchemical preparations. Circulation provokes the evolution of the matter towards a more perfect state. Tall wine bottles filled with only three or four ounces and set on a warm heating pad will work for this.

CALCINATION

Calcination takes its name from the word calx, which is an old term meaning lime or quicklime (calcium oxide) which is a white powder. When something is calcined we apply fire to produce a white ash (usually) by burning away the various volatile constituents and revealing the essential mineral components -- the Salt.

Burning herbs to ash is easy enough over a small propane stove, but there are a few problems. First there is the smoke and smell, sure to attract the attention of your neighbors and elicit moans and groans from other people of your household. Unless you have a good fume hood, this is definitely an outdoor activity. Secondly, there are some materials which refuse to get very white at all. There is a simple method we can use, called the leaching process, to obtain the salts in a purified form.

After extracting your herb with alcohol, the plant residue is filtered out and placed into a heat-resistant dish. (Metal dishes are OK, but avoid aluminum.) Take it outside and place it on a brick or some other fire-resistant holder. Then touch a match to it. Let the herb burn and stir it around once in a while to burn as much as possible. It should turn black and if you are lucky it will calcine by itself to gray. A small propane camp stove is perfect for many operations used in alchemy.

Once the plant has been reduced to a gray ash, grind it and continue calcining to get it light gray. Prolonged calcining and grinding will eventually give you a very light gray to almost white ash. To speed this up we can take our gray ash and mix it with ten to twenty times its volume of water. Shake it or stir it well. You can even heat it up to near boiling, then filter and collect the liquid. Place the liquid in a bowl and allow it to evaporate under a gentle heat. A white crystalline material will remain, collect this, grind it fine and keep it dry. This is called the *Salt of Salt*. The material that remains in the filter (which did not dissolve in the water) is called the *Caput Mortuum* or Dead Head also called *Terra Damnata* or Damned Earth and is usually discarded.

There is another salt we obtain from plants. In working, you will notice that many plants do not give a lot of volatile oil, the Alchemical Sulfur. They are said to have a Fixed Sulfur. For these we can take the fermentation liquor (after removal of the alcohol, our Mercury) or an alcohol extract of the plant, evaporate it to a thick honey-like mass, then calcine it. It will turn black and continued calcination may get it to gray but generally not.

It stays black so we use a little trick to help. Grind the black material then wet it with distilled water or better yet, the collected *phlegm* of the plant, just to saturation. Let it stand overnight, then gently calcine it again. You will notice that it becomes lighter. Repeat this process of wetting and calcining several times and you will slowly bring it to a very light gray or even to white. This can now be leached out with water as you did for the plant ash, filter and crystallize it. This will give us the *Salt of Sulfur*, which is a magnet for the subtle principle of Sulfur of the particular plant.

In almost all cases you will find that a long slow calcination works better than a short violent one.

SOLVE *et* COAGULA

This is an ancient alchemical formula for exalting our matter. In herbal work it is applied to the salts we collected and from the standpoint of chemistry it is a simple recrystallization where our salts are dissolved into water, filtered and again evaporated to dryness. From the alchemical viewpoint we are passing our matter through the life, death and rebirth cycle.

In the liquid state materials are much more susceptible to astrological influences (especially through the Moon) and we use this to impress or augment a planetary power in our subject. It is not uncommon to repeat this process of *solve et coagula* a number of times using distilled water or a specially prepared type of water which has already captured certain astrological influences during its manufacture. With each cycle, the subject becomes more powerful.

' An excellent source of this water is the so-called *Phlegm* from distilling and rectifying the alcohol. This phlegm is obtained by continuing the distillation (after removal of the alcohol) of our fermentation liquid down to the thickened honey-like residue from which we obtain the Salt of Sulfur. The water that distills over is called the Phlegm and it is held to be the best solvent for purifying the salts of the body it was derived from; so keep it aside until needed.

As fire is the active agent for purification of spiritual energies (niter), water is the active agent for purification of material energies (salt).

These are just a few of the common operations of laboratory alchemy, and these in turn are related to the planets or signs of the zodiac under whose influence they are preferentially performed.

Remember that there is also the inner alchemy, which affects the operator as well. Each of these operations can become a very powerful transformative meditation during their performance if we consciously relate ourselves with our subject matter. For example, during the calcinations of our plant material, we burn off the volatile structural components of the plant, which served to protect it from the environment and ensure its propagation during its life. These components are no longer necessary as it enters a new phase in its life as an evolved alchemical elixir in the service of the alchemist. Similarly within our psyche we have accumulated various ephemeral components in the mask of our personality (some good some bad), which have served their purpose and are no longer required.

There are many things we have tucked away deep in our unconscious that we prefer to forget about altogether and it takes a good deal of our energy to keep them hidden (though they have a habit of popping out from time to time) and this is energy blocked up in a useless waste that is better used elsewhere.

We've all been in "the hot seat" during our lives when these things we try to hide and hope they will go away, do come out. Or we have more catastrophic events which rip our lives apart and we are forced to look deeply within to determine what really is most essential in our lives. This is part of our personal calcination.

We can consciously pull these things out, examine them for what they are, learn from them, defuse the grip they have on us due to erroneous beliefs, and move on. In this way we purposely calcine out those parts of the psyche which tie up energy. We free this energy for our own personal transformation into our True Selves.

So it is with each of the alchemical operations. There is a corresponding internal process that leads to our own transformation into an evolved being. Very often it is not easy nor a comfortable thing or a pretty sight. That is why it is called the Great Work. But in the end, the things that have kept us as heavy as lead become transmuted into incorruptible spiritual gold.

The processes of laboratory alchemy have a strange way of working on us at all levels in spite of ourselves. As we work on our matter it is working on us.

The Zodiac and Alchemical Operations.

The various stages our matter must pass through on its way to becoming perfected by Art will be dependent on the particular subject of the work. Alchemy recognizes twelve of the most common chemical operations, one for each sign of the Zodiac. When the Moon is in a particular constellation a corresponding

chemical operation is performed. In other words, the subtle
energies governing the operation or state of the matter to be
operated on are considered to be optimal or at least active.

The Operations and the Zodiac Signs are classically listed as
follows:

PLANET	SIGN	ELEMENT	DURATION	OPERATION
Mars +	Aries	Fire	Cardinal	Digestion
Venus -	Taurus	Earth	Fixed	Fixation
Mercury +	Gemini	Air	Mutable	Distillation
Moon +/-	Cancer	Water	Cardinal	Separation
Sun +/-	Leo	Fire	Fixed	Calcination
Mercury -	Virgo	Earth	Mutable	Congelation
Venus +	Libra	Air	Cardinal	Sublimation
Mars -	Scorpio	Water	Fixed	Dissolution
Jupiter +	Sagittarius	Fire	Mutable	Incineration
Saturn -	Capricorn	Earth	Cardinal	Fermentation
Saturn +	Aquarius	Air	Fixed	Multiplying
Jupiter -	Pisces	Water	Mutable	Projection

CHAPTER SIX

Herbal Alchemy

Now we come to the point of actually applying these processes to prepare various Spagyric and alchemical products. We described the preparation of the "Seven Basics" as a prelude or first step on the alchemical path. There are many different ways to obtain the Three Essentials and many preparations for use along the alchemical path -- each with unique medicinal and initiatory powers. We have talked about Tinctures and Elixirs, now we are going to explore several others with colorful names and surprisingly powerful effects.

The Magisteries

The process for producing the so-called *Magistery* of a plant has several variations. This one comes to us from Paracelsus. It is fairly simple, and requires only a distillation setup, some fresh herb, and a little 190 proof alcohol. We can produce seven magisteries from different plants each ruled by one of the planets, just as we did for the Seven Basics.

The process requires a series of digestions and distillations which volatilize the three essentials followed by a final circulation. Here is the method:

Take a fresh plant and chop it up a bit. Put it into a container and pour your alcohol over it until the herb is covered. This should be rectified spirit of wine but any strong (potable) alcohol will work. Seal it, then let it digest at about 40°C for one month. Then, take the matter and gently distill it in a water bath until it is dry. (Be careful not to burn it.) Pour this distillate (which now contains the liquid of the plant as well as the alcohol you started with) over some fresh herb and again digest at 40°C for a month. Distill the whole again and collect the distillate which will have increased in volume again.

Repeat this process of digesting fresh herb in the distillate for a month and distilling until the volume is five times the original volume of alcohol used. If we used 100ml alcohol to start, we will end up with 500ml total at the end. Circulate this final distillate for one month, after which time the Magistery will collect as oily-looking drops and either sink to the bottom or float on top, depending on the herb's nature. Collect this with a dropper into a small vial and keep it sealed well.

Paracelsus says one part of this Magistery has the same effect as two hundred times the quantity of the corresponding dried plant (so 1/2oz = 100oz).

The Ens

In his work entitled "Paramirim," Paracelsus describes five powers which form the root causes of disease in man. These powers, which he terms *Ens* (or *Entia* in the plural) are subtle influences, spiritual yet involved in physical causation.

The so-called *Ens Tinctures* are held to be effective at these subtle levels and considered by many to be among the most powerful Spagyric medicines which can be used to correct our own imbalances, bringing us to a state of physical and spiritual health in a much more powerful way than the Seven Basics. One modern operator writes:

> "The Ens manifests the highest initiatic virtue of the plant it is made from. Since alchemy has no set rituals, no lodges, or methods of advancement other than the

Work itself, all initiation is said to be interior in this form of esotericism. We initiate ourselves into the Work, and the Work initiates us to higher (and deeper) levels of awareness.

The nature of spagyric tinctures, and in particular the Ens, is to clear out the blocks in our psychic makeup and anatomy, similar to what is called Nadis in yoga or the Meridians in acupuncture. This subtle anatomy allows for the exchange of information between the dense physical world of matter, and the subtler psychic world of which it is an extension."

-- Mark Stavish, "Practical Plant Alchemy," 1998

The simplest Ens Tinctures are prepared from herbs, and like our Seven Basics or Magisteries, one can be made for each of the seven planetary rulers, for each day of the week.

The preparation of the ENS Tincture is only a bit more complicated than our simple Spagyric elixirs, and yet their effect is held to be comparable to an elixir which has greater maturity and potency. The simple skills we learn from this experiment will serve us in future works upon the mineral realm.

There are a number of methods suggested for preparing an ENS Tincture, the following method is perhaps the most common. It derives from the works of Paracelsus and specifically from a commentary on his life and works by Franz Hartman.

Preparing The ENS Tincture

The same materials are used as previously described for making the Seven Basics. The alcohol must be very strong, not less than 95%. In addition, one or two pounds of potassium

carbonate will be needed, and a wide glass dish like those used for baking.

Potassium carbonate can be purchased from a chemical supply shop or you can also find it at a ceramics supply, often under the name of "pearl ash" for substantially less cost. In the old days, potassium carbonate was known as the *Salt of Tartar*.

If you like, you can collect potassium carbonate the old way by leaching it from wood ashes (especially oak wood, grape vine, and fern ash.) This will give you something to do with all those ashes you clean out of your fireplace or woodstove. Just scoop them out and place them into a large plastic bucket. Pour clean water over them (tap water is fine) stir and let settle. Pour off the clear liquid from the top, filter and evaporate the water. Be careful, because it is quite caustic and can burn the skin and seriously injure your eyes. It is like lye (in fact it is lye) and they used to make soap this way.

After the water evaporates you will have a crystalline mass that is more or less white. You can set this in your broiler for a while to get it white. Let this crystalline material sit outside protected from dust and rain late in the evening till early morning several nights in a row and you will see that a large part of it will have turned into liquid by absorbing the moisture from the air. This is called *Deliquescence*.

Collect all of this liquid you can and evaporate the water from it in a clean dish. This will give you a crude potassium carbonate. You can calcine this, dissolve it in water, then recrystallize it several times to make it pure.

This takes quite a bit of time and patience, but it is free and the end product can be used over and over again. Over time you can gather a fairly large amount of material which can be used for a number of different alchemical works and, in addition, gain some valuable experience in the manipulation of salts.

Spread the potassium carbonate in a thin layer inside a glass dish, no more than one quarter of an inch thick. Again, care should be taken to avoid exposure to the potassium carbonate in either its dry or liquefied state. So be sure to wash your hands thoroughly after handling to avoid any contamination, especially of your eyes which can be seriously damaged. The potassium carbonate is strong enough to etch the sides of the glass container used during this experiment so do not use anything you value. It will likely be destroyed.

Place the dish in an area where it will be exposed to the night air. As the potassium carbonate liquefies (becomes deliquescent) it absorbs the moisture carried in the air. This moisture is said to be the vehicle of a *Universal Fire* or *Vital Force* which is most easily obtained in the Spring and early Summer months. We'll have much more to say about this later. Draw off the liquid as it accumulates into a clean container. This liquid is called the ***Oil of Tartar per Deliquium***.

When several ounces of liquid have been collected, you can begin the extraction procedure. It is best to filter the liquid through a ball of cotton or glass wool prior to use. Paper filters absorb a lot of the liquid and tend to fall apart due to the corrosive nature of the fluid.

Place about two ounces of finely ground herb in a clean, dry jar and pour in the clear fluid you have collected and filtered. Beginning this operation when the planet ruling the herb is in a powerful position will assist you in your Work. Pour in enough fluid to cover the top of the herb until it becomes a fully liquefied mass. Also allow space for thorough shaking, and seal with a tight plastic lid.

Digest for a week or two with periodic shaking. The liquid will become darkly colored during this time. Carefully squeeze the mixture through a nylon stocking and place the liquid into a clean vessel. Remember to use gloves and eye protection for this.

Now pour in an equal amount of strong alcohol (at least 95%) and shake daily to insure the two liquids mix, as the lighter alcohol will float on top. If the two liquids do not separate, it means there was too much water in the herb or the alcohol. Slowly add solid dry potassium carbonate to absorb the excess water. If separation does not occur, you will have to start again.

The alcohol extract floating on top will be the Ens Tincture that will be removed after the digestion. The alcohol will become darkly tinted after a few days. After about two weeks (or longer) you can carefully draw off the alcohol tincture from the top of the Oil of Tartar / herb layer. Allow it to stand for a day or two then filter for use.

It is helpful to let it stand in a freezer during this time, so that any water containing dissolved potassium carbonate will tend to crystallize out more easily. You will want to get the best separation of the two liquids as possible. Remember to save the Oil of Tartar for future use. It can be dried, calcined and used again.

In general, five to ten drops of the Ens Tincture is taken in a glass of wine or water on the day ruled by the planet of the herb. It will have an effect on the subtle or astral body of the user, as well as enhanced medicinal qualities of the particular plant. Take note of both physical effects and how it affects your habitual thought and emotional patterns.

The Primum Ens Melissa

Perhaps the most well-known Ens extract is the *Primum Ens Melissa*. Paracelsus mentions the herb Melissa with high praise and says it is loaded with an easily obtained *Quintessence* of great rejuvenating virtue.

Franz Hartman mentions an often-quoted case of its use by Lesebure, a physician of Louis XIV of France, who gives in his "Guide to Chemistry" (written about 1685) an account of some experiments, witnessed by him:

"One of my most intimate friends prepared the Primum Ens Melissae, and his curiosity would not allow him to rest until he had seen with his own eyes the effect of this arcanum, so that he might be certain whether or not the accounts given of its virtues were true. He therefore made the experiment, first upon himself then upon an old female servant, aged seventy years, and afterwards upon an old hen that was kept at his house. First he took, every morning at sunrise, a glass of white wine that was tinctured with this remedy, and after using it for fourteen days his finger and toenails began to fall out, without, however, causing any pain. He was not courageous enough to continue the experiment, but gave the same remedy to the old female servant. She took it every morning for about ten days, when she began to menstruate again as in former days. At this she was very much surprised, because she did not know that she had been taking a medicine. She became frightened, and refused to continue the experiment. My friend took, therefore, some grain, soaked it in that wine and gave it to the old hen to eat, and on the sixth day that bird began to lose its feathers, and kept on losing them until it was perfectly nude, but before two weeks had passed away, new feathers grew, which were much more beautifully coloured; her comb stood up again, and she began again to lay eggs".

The Vegetable Stone

The preparation of the Vegetable Stone has been called the **Opus Minor**, the Little Work or Lesser Circulation (in comparison to the **Magnum Opus** -- the Great Work of the Philosopher's Stone.)

In the creation of a "Stone" in the Vegetable Kingdom, we seek to balance the Elements of an herb in their most exalted form, which represents the true Quintessence of the plant.

The effects of the Stone are quite powerful, both at the physical level and at the energetic level. Like the Ens Tinctures, the Vegetable Stone is held to possess an initiatic virtue that can bring an awareness of Nature's operations by opening the subtle energy flow between our "interior stars." They also represent a sort of merit badge marking the progress of the alchemist's mastery over the vegetable realm and his own lower nature.

Creating an Herbal Stone takes some time. It could easily take a year or longer and if you do not start with enough material, you end up with only a small amount. Plan to use ten to fifty pounds of herb depending on which herb you choose. Prefer plants where you can easily collect a good quantity of essential oils and that provide ample amounts of salts after calcination.

The method we are going to examine provides the basic operations common to many of the ways of making a Stone. There are many variations possible and the actual process that you use will be uniquely yours. It may be called the Little Work, but it does take some work and this method is most often successful.

The first part of this work is the separation and purification of your Three Essentials. Ideally you would steam distill out the essential oil, then ferment the plant and distill out the alcohol, followed by multiple redistillations to obtain a very pure product. The remaining plant residue is calcined and the salts obtained by leaching. This will give you the *Salt of Salt*.

The liquid remaining from the fermentation and removal of the alcohol is evaporated and calcined also. This will provide the *Salt of Sulfur* which can also be obtained by leaching the calcined residue as we mentioned earlier.

The Solar Fire can be increased in the salts by setting them outside at night to deliquesce. Leave the salts to dry in the Sun. In this way, as they crystallize they absorb and trap more of the Sun's energy.

Take the salts inside and grind them fine, then place them into a Pyrex dish. Place the dish into an oven at a temperature of two hundred to three hundred degrees Celsius. This roasting of the salts causes their "pores" to open, as the old artists would say.

Take the still-warm salts out of the oven and place them in a warm mortar. Grind the salts fine. Pour the salts into a vial in an even layer. Pour enough of the essential oil over the salts so that they are just saturated. Seal the vial and place it in anincubator at 40°C. There the salts should remain undisturbed for a week.

On the appropriate day of the following week check the salts. If they have absorbed all of the oil, add some more. When the same amount of oil remains on the top of your salts as you put in a week before, the salts have taken up all they can hold.

Begin adding your alcohol in the same manner as you did the oil. Keep the process up until no more alcohol will go into the salts. When this is done your stone is finished to the *First Degree*.

You can increase the virtue of your stone by grinding it and subjecting it to a gentle distillation and calcination of the residue. Grind the salts again and return the distillate to them with additions of fresh oil and alcohol as needed. You can repeat this process several times and in the end you will have a powerful medicine.

You can mature your Stone by allowing it to digest in the heat of the incubator for six months to a year. If it appears to dry out, continue adding fresh oil and alcohol in equal amounts to keep it moist. If done properly, the matter will congeal to a hardened stone which will work to separate the essentials from a macerating herb simply by immersing it in the herb / water mixture. The herb's Salt, Sulfur, and Mercury will gather together as a layer floating on the water surface, from which it is collected for use without any further preparation. The Stone is recovered unharmed for further use. This use of the stone is not nearly as efficient as a "circulatum" which forms our last topic of study. If not fully matured, the stone will fall apart upon immersion in water. It can be very disheartening to see months of work dissolve before your eyes. Many operators don't attempt this experiment and utilize the stone only as a powerful medicine.

In using the Stone medicinally, a small amount is taken in a little water or wine. The effects are related to the Stone's planetary ruler and can open doors of perception to its particular sphere, providing lasting insight to the various realms we have been discussing. The effect on the general health can be astonishing and quite overpowering. This is the reason that preliminary purification of the artist using preparations such as the Seven Basics is highly recommended.

Circulatum Minus

The so-called *circulatum* is essentially a liquid version of the plant stone which acts as a powerful menstrum or solvent in the extraction of plants. The most concise description of its preparation comes to us from a small book first published in 1690 by Baron Urbigerus, entitled *Circulatum Minus Urbigeranum.*

As with the vegetable stone, preparation of the circulatum depends on the marriage of the three essentials derived from the plant and purified prior to their recombination.

In practice, a fairly large amount of salt of salt, and salt of sulfur are required since the final volume of circulatum will depend on their combined volume.

The combined salts are fully saturated with the essential oil and digested at 40 degrees C for several weeks. Additional oil may be required during the digestion and the whole should be stirred often until it becomes of a thick honey like consistency. Unlike the vegetable stone, the circulatum uses an excess of the volatile components; that is to say, the amount of volatiles is always greater than the fixed salts.

Urbigerus recommends addition of **Bituminous Sulfur** to this mixture in order to aid volatilization of the salts, which is the key to this preparation.

This bituminous sulfur is derived from the resin of the particular plant or that derived from another plant in which it is more plentiful. Urbigerus recommends Copaivian Balsam, but other sources include, pine, cedar, yew, and Canadian Balsam. Add just enough to thicken the matter and solublize the salts to the honey like consistency. The organic acids present in the resin assist in volatilizing the salts so that they will distill over united with the alcohol later.

After the period of digestion, add rectified alcohol at six to eight times the volume of your matter, seal and let digest at 40 degrees C for another two weeks to a month.

Now the flask is attached to a distillation train and gently distilled down to the honey like consistency again. Be careful not to push the fire too high and drive the sulfur over, or burn the matter.

Take all of the clear distillate and pour it back over the matter in the flask, seal and digest again for two weeks. After this, distill again. This process is called circulation and the cycle must be repeated seven to twelve times to complete the preparation.

The final distillate should be clear and have a sharp penetrating odor quite unlike the original alcohol. This is now the Circulatum.

In use, the circulatum is generally poured over a fresh, finely shredded plant and shaken. The liquid may become milky looking depending on the quantity and qualities of the plant's oils. The extracted plant residue will fall to the bottom and the milky emulsion will coalesce into drops of oily liquid that rise to the surface. This oily liquid contains the essentials of the plant, including its salts, so carefully collect it and save for use. The circulatum is recovered from the residue and gently distilled for use in other extractions. Its power is said to increase the more it is used.

CHAPTER SEVEN

Water Works

Practical Alchemy, as an experimental art and science, provides a means of exploring the works of Nature and gaining first hand knowledge of these operations. The old masters were often called *Chemical Philosophers*, and they understood the essential unity of all creation. By exploring materials in the laboratory, they came to an understanding of the more subtle realms preceding the physical manifestation.

Aside from the quest for the Philosophers Stone, there are many interesting paths to explore and each one sheds light on another as we learn to work with Nature. The alchemist provides Nature with the proper materials and conditions, then Nature is all too happy to bring them to their fruition. As one Sage wrote:

> "Nature and Art must assist each other to perfect the works; Art operates without, and Nature within the glass."

> -- F. la Fontain, "Curious Aphorisms Concerning the Universal Salt of Nature," 1797

Volatile and Fixed Solvents

We spoke of the initial division of the One into a volatile / spiritual aspect and a fixed / material aspect. The Sulfur exhibits the fire and air qualities of the volatile aspect while Salt exhibits the water and earth qualities of the fixed. The Mercury acts in both worlds and can be of a fixed or volatile nature.

On the practical level we use a Mercury to extract or separate the essentials of our matter and this can be with a fixed solvent or a volatile one. In general, a volatile solvent evaporates more rapidly than water. A fixed solvent evaporates less quickly than water, but in alchemy it is their action upon our subject matter which shows their real difference.

In Herbal Alchemy, we use the alcohol as our volatile solvent and produce what is called an unfixed tincture. If instead, we extract our plant with vinegar, we will obtain a fixed tincture because we used a fixed solvent -- vinegar.

In winemaking, the plant dies and its spirit enters the watery medium as the alcohol. If we leave this open, the wine will go through a second death as the wine becomes vinegar which fixes the spirit. These two spirits, one fixed and one volatile, lie at the heart of practical alchemical work in the herbal realm and the mineral realm.

Medicinally, the volatile or unfixed elixirs are warming, energizing and toning in their effects, while the fixed elixirs are cooling and contracting. Unfixed tinctures are said to be more effective in acute illnesses while fixed tinctures are more useful for chronic diseases.

"Remedies that are unfixed heal unfixed diseases and the radically fixed nonvolatile ones expel fixed diseases which do not move the excrements through evacuation but through sweating and by other means."
-- Isaac Newton "Keynes Ms. 64"

70

Water Work

There are some experiments we can do which lie at a borderline between the Vegetable and Mineral worlds.
One very interesting area concerns the use of salts as "magnets" for subtle forces which then become available for our work in the laboratory. Another, which we will examine first, is the work upon water itself.

Water is a strange creature. It is the only substance on our planet that exists in solid, liquid and gaseous states at the same time under the normal range of temperatures and pressures we experience.

As mentioned earlier, the Sun radiates the vital energies throughout our Solar System. This *Universal Fire* of life is one of the alchemist's *Secret Fires*. As this spiritual fire hits our atmosphere, it condenses in the air and is carried by it. As the air fills with moisture, the Universal Fire condenses even further and moves into the water. The water gathers and it starts to rain.

This water, charged with the Secret Fire (a Universal Mercury) becomes *determined* for use by a particular kingdom when it hits the Earth. If it falls on plants, it is determined to the Vegetable Kingdom. If touched or drunk by man or animal, it is determined to the Animal Kingdom and if it strikes the Earth, it is determined to the Mineral Kingdom.

"The Golden Chain of Homer" provides one of the clearest descriptions of this process. The text describes the Universal Fire generating "an invisible and most subtle humidity" which consequently undergoes a gentle fermentation to generate the Universal Acid – "a most subtle, spiritual Incorporeal Niter Spiritus Mundi." As this Universal Acid enters the atmosphere, it becomes more material and meets an Alkaline, passive principle, whereupon it becomes fixed as native Niter.

In modern practical alchemy, the element Hydrogen is attributed to Fire, Nitrogen to Air, Oxygen to Water, and Carbon to the Earth element. The other material elements of the respective periods in the periodic table share these qualities as well.

71

Hydrogen is the most abundant element in the universe, a true *First Matter*, and is the first carrier of the Fire while Nitrogen possesses the most oxidation states of any element and is said to "coagulate matter."

These two form the Fire and Air group which the ancients called Alkali (NH_3, ammonia) and later become the matrix of the ammonium (NH_4) salts.

The second group of atmospheric constituents is the "Acid Niter" group or Fire / Air / Water group ($H_2/N_2/O_2$) from which niter originates. The acid niter (HNO_3) is ammonia to which the element of Water has been added.

The *Spirit of the World*, the Embodied Alkali, is in the Ammonium (NH_4) radical. This is often called Sal Ammoniac and is deposited as rain, snow, dew and hail over the Earth. It is carried in the water as the *Salt of Dew* or Ammonium Nitrate (NH_4NO_3) at about 0.5 to 4 grams per ton of rain.

The practical work mentioned in "The Golden Chain of Homer" provides a method of capturing the *Universal Seed of Nature*, of determining this seed, and growing it to its ultimate perfection using only rainwater.

From the *Mutus Liber*

REAL ALCHEMY

We begin by collecting rainwater. This is done in a special way. First of all, this operation is best performed during the Spring when the Sun is in Aries, Taurus, or Gemini and thundershowers are preferred since the lightning fixes more nitrogen in the air. And secondly, the rain should not touch metal, the Earth or plants or animals (including human contact.)

The operation is easily done by staking out a piece of plastic sheeting and leading the runoff into a catch bottle or plastic bucket. (It is good to filter all the water collected.) Cover the container with a piece of cloth to keep dust out but let the water "breathe."

Place it in a warm spot (30° to 40°C) to ferment for at least a month, but longer is better. Some wait a year or even more. At the end of this time you should see white to brownish solid-like tufts of cotton floating in the water. This is the *Universal Gur* or *Seed of Nature*.

Place all of the water (including the Gur) into a distillation apparatus and very gently sweat over the first quarter of its volume. Label this distillate as the *Fire and Air of Water*. Raise the temperature and continue the distillation until most of the water has come over but not to dryness. Label this distillate *Water of Water*. The residue which remains is placed into a dish and slowly allowed to dry in the Sun, labeled as *Earth of Water* and contains the Universal Gur.

The text continues with instructions for moistening the Earth with various proportions of the Fire, Air, and Water fractions to generate Mineral, Vegetable, or Animal life in the Gur. It is said that the Universal Seed can be *determined* in order to grow any specified form to maturity.

All of Nature comes from seed. Alchemy has often been described as a "Celestial Agriculture."

The Seven-fold or 4x3 Distillation

Another common method of separating the Elements of Water is called a Seven-fold distillation or 4X3 distillation.
The fermented water is first distilled gently into four equal volumes. The first quarter to distill is labeled as *Fire of Water*. The second quarter is labeled as *Air of Water*. Next comes the Water Element followed by Earth. Again, the distillation is stopped before dryness and the residue is dried then labeled as the Gur.

Now take each collected quarter in turn and distill it into three parts which come over in the order Sulfur, Mercury, and Salt. For example, the Fire fraction is placed into the still and gently heated. The first third to distill over is the *Sulfur of Fire of Water*, the next third is *Mercury of Fire of Water*. The remaining third is labeled *Salt of Fire of Water*.

At the end of this process you will have twelve fractions representing the Body, Soul, and Spirit of each of the Four Elements.

These twelve fractions can be combined in various proportions to moisten the Gur as in the previous operation. Each of these twelve fractions from water is said to possess unique medicinal properties on their own and being twelve in number, they have been given astrological correspondences.

These correspondences are properly derived from the Cardinal, Fixed and Mutable signs of each Element. Cardinal relates to the fiery Sulfur, Mutable to the mediating nature of Mercury and Fixed to the principle of Salt. For example, our Fire of Water was distilled into the following thirds:

Sulfur of Fire of Water—Aries
Mercury of Fire of Water—Sagittarius
Salt of Fire of Water -- Leo

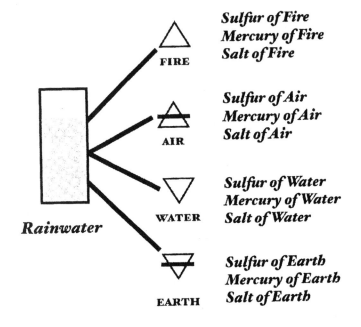

It is said that by the proper manipulation of these water experiments one can even grow and multiply metallic gold much as is done with any vegetable seed crop. Although it is not commonly known, the alchemists understood the Mineral realm to have its own form of seed just as the Vegetable and Animal worlds have their unique forms of seed. We'll come back to this idea later.

The various works on water can be quite educational with regard to the operations of Nature and lead to some surprising results. The work itself requires some labor in distilling because a fairly large volume of rain is needed at the beginning, but it is an inherently "safe" alchemical work (there are no toxic materials used) and is available to anyone.

The Salts

A related line of operations (capturing the *Universal Fire* into a corporeal form) is the work with salts. By the use of certain properties of selected salts we can capture and concentrate this vital, Universal Fire for our alchemical work of evolving our matter and ourselves. These salts form the basis for many of the *Secret Fires* mentioned in alchemical texts. These act as a catalyst in the operation to effect separation or conjunction of principles.

> "The secrets of the ancients are in the salts. The magnetic salts should attract and capture the steel, the astral spirit, the universal seed, which, once concentrated, gives the germination power directed in accordance to the matrix in which it was incorporated."

> --Jean Dubuis (PON Seminars 1992)

There are a number of mineral and metallic salts which have a long association with the alchemical art.   The fifteenth century alchemist, Isaac Holland describes *The Hand of the Philosophers* as being an assembly of important salts in alchemical works. These salts include Niter (potassium nitrate), Sal Ammoniac (ammonium chloride), Vitriol (copper or iron sulfate), Alum (potassium aluminum sulfate), and common salt (sodium chloride).

Through their proper combinations and manipulation, anything can be made to yield its spiritualized essence.

Holland describes them as keys to unlock matter. In his commentary to Basil Valentine's "Triumphal Chariot of Antimony," Dr Theodor Kerkring says:

> "Salts are keys; they open the chest wherein the treasure lies but you must be sure to take the true key; otherwise you may spoil the lock and not open the chest."

77

Later on when we discuss mineral and metallic works, we'll get more deeply involved with salts. For these beginning operations of capturing *Celestial Fire* we will examine several common salts and how they are used in this process. In each case, it is the Salt's ability to *deliquesce* in the air that is utilized.

> "Few persons know how to extract from the rays of the Sun or of the Moon. The means to make this water to descend from Heaven is truly wonderful; it is in the stone which contains the Central Water, which is indeed one sole and the same thing with the Celestial Water, but the secret consists in the knowing how to make the stone a magnet to attract, embrace, and unite this Astral Quintessence to itself".
>
> "Hermetical Triumph" 1723

Mutus Liber

Salt of Tartar

We talked about this when we described the process for creating an Ens Tincture. The *Salt of Tartar* is potassium carbonate derived from the calcination of wine tartar or plant ashes and provides an easily obtained starting material for many works.

Spread the salt in a thin layer (1/4 to 1/2 in.) in a glass baking dish. Set the dish of salt outside, protected from rain and dust, but exposed to the air. Do this in the late evening until six or seven A.M. This is accomplished even better in the Spring when the Sun is in Aries, Taurus, or Gemini because there is more of the Universal Fire with generative force present.

The salt will deliquesce, or become liquefied, by absorbing the moisture of the air which is loaded with the condensed Universal Fire -- the Secret Fire. This liquid, called the *Oil of Tartar per Deliquiem*, was used in the Ens extraction. Remember, this liquid is quite caustic and will burn the skin and especially the eyes, so be careful with it.

Another use of it is to gently distill the liquid just to dryness. The clear, watery distillate has been called *Angel Water* and can be used in the recrystallization of the herbal salts. This liquid, loaded with the Secret Fire, becomes enmeshed with the crystalline matrix of the salts as they crystallize, thus revivifying them. This type of transference of subtle force always takes place in the liquid state, thus the Alchemists stressed Solution as one of the important stages in the work. The volatile becomes fixed and the fixed becomes volatile. The dried potassium carbonate can be recovered and reused.

The liquid distillate is also useful in plant extractions. It is said to be determined to the Vegetable World, because of the salt's prevalence in plant ashes, and thus useful for all work in the herbal realm. Just as the potassium salts are said to carry the Vegetable Fire, sodium salts carry the Fire in the Animal World. These elements lie in the same period as Hydrogen (the Fire element) in the Periodic Table, but at more densified levels.

We can use common salt in the above experiment to obtain water charged with Animal Fire. Salt (NaCl) will not deliquesce but can absorb a significant quantity of moisture. Use pure dried sea salt to which nothing has been added for this. The yield is much smaller but just as powerful for work in the Animal realm.

Dew Salt

Another salt often worked with in the same way and mentioned earlier is called Dew Salt, or *The Heavenly Dew Salt*. It can be derived from collected dew or rainwater (especially that collected during a thundershower) but this is long and tedious. The salt itself is ammonium nitrate. The Dew Salt is highly deliquescent and said to be determined to the Mineral realm especially, but it is of a Universal nature. Sometimes, you can find this salt in gardening stores as a fertilizer, but it is becoming harder to find because of its use in creating makeshift explosives.

There really is a lot of fire in this salt! It can be prepared by mixing nitric acid and ammonium hydroxide until neutral, then crystallizing. Solve Et Coagula a few times by deliquescence to revivify. Be careful with this salt too, it is a powerful oxidizer and can ignite various types of fuel materials.

Distillation of this salt when it liquefies is stopped well before the dry point. Crystals will form which can be reused. This distillate can be used in various operations in the Mineral work in place of distilled water.

This distillate is loaded with the Mineral Fire, which can be transferred to our subject in order to reanimate it. Copper salts also carry Mineral Fire as copper is part of the group 1B elements in the Periodic Table, and thus related to the elements under Hydrogen, all of which are carriers of the Fire.

Butter of Antimony

The last salt we'll mention in this category is antimony trichloride, also called *Butter of Antimony*. Properly, this belongs to the Mineral works so we will only mention its use at this point. The preparation and use of this salt is much more difficult and dangerous than any of the salts previously discussed. When it is prepared, it has the color and texture of butter, hence the name. However, it is toxic and very corrosive so it requires some skill and practice to work with safely.

The Butter of Antimony has a ravenous appetite for the moisture in the air and will deliquesce even on a hot sunny day. The water distilled from it is said to carry a truly Universal Fire which can be set to operate in any of the three kingdoms.

The Archaeus of Water

Some operators combine the above methods to produce a reconstituted water called the *Archaeus of Water*. It is an evolved form of water with surprising medicinal effects.

The water obtained by deliquescence of a salt is loaded with Fire and considered the male / Sulfur / Sun aspect, while the rain or snow waters are considered to represent the female / Mercury / Lunar aspect of the *Celestial Waters*.

A quantity of collected rainwater (the female) is "impregnated" with the distilled *Angel Water* (the male), then allowed to ferment for at least a month. After fermentation, the water is separated using the 4X3 distillation described above.

Once the twelve fractions of water have been obtained, the process of recombination can begin. Starting with the Fire element, equal volumes of the Sulfur, Mercury, and Salt fractions are combined, then allowed to circulate for several days. Let it cool, then set it aside for later use. Repeat this process on each of the remaining elements until you obtain the four elements in their reconstituted form.

Now combine equal volumes from each of these elements and allow this to circulate for a week to a month at about 40°C. Notice we do not use the Gur in this preparation. The resulting *Celestial Water* is called the *Archaeus or First Being of Water*, and can be used as a solvent for extractions in any realm or as a healing water on its own.

The Archaeus represents a Universal Mercury, and can be determined for operation in any of the three realms by adjusting the relative proportions of the four elements during its preparation. The four elements of water should be present in each Archaeus, but not equally as we did above. If the Earth element is predominant, the Archaeus will be determined to the Metallic realm. If the elements of Earth and Water predominate, the Archaeus will be determined to the Mineral realm. Water and Air predominant will determine it to the Vegetable realm, while Fire and Air will determine the Animal realm. The mixtures are circulated as before, then they are ready for use.

The dried Gur we collected is placed into a flask, then moistened / impregnated with the Archaeus. Close the flask and digest. (At about 40°C for Vegetable works or up to about 90°C for Mineral / Metal works.) Continue just moistening the Gur as it dries out.

If you prepared an Archaeus determined to the Vegetable Realm, you should see primitive plant life appear after some time. Keep it moistened. As soon as this plant appears to die, calcine the material and add the ashes to fresh Gur. Now begin the process of imbibing the Gur with the Archaeus again. After some time, a new and more evolved plant life should appear. This whole operation can be repeated as often as desired in order to observe the progression of the plant life.

If instead, you prepared an Archaeus determined to the Mineral Realm, the moistened Gur will at first become gritty, like sand and pass through various colors. It is said that if the proportions are correct, you may even develop a few grains of gold and silver.

These operations with water are generally long-term. They require some labor at first and long times for digestion. Like trying to cultivate a rare orchid, success may require you to make several attempts. They do provide some interesting experience and insight to alchemical work wherein "Nature is assisted by Art."

CHAPTER EIGHT

Return to the Fire

Let us return to our discussion of fire which began with common fire, only now we are going to examine some of the more subtle aspects of Fire presented in alchemical texts. Nature has its degrees of volatility and fixity. Alchemy really is all about the Fire in its various aspects.

"Fire is the primary agent, that of the whole Art. It is the first of the Four Elements."
                                        --Olympiodorus, circa 500 C.E.

"Fire, notwithstanding the diversities of it in this sub-lunary kitchen of the elements, is but one thing from one root. This fire is at the root and about the root -- I mean about the center of all things both visible and invisible. It is in water, earth and air, it is in minerals, herbs and beasts; it is in men, stars and angels. But originally it is in God Himself; for He is the fountain of heat and fire, and from Him it is derived to the rest of the creatures in a certain stream of sunshine"

> -- Dr. John Dee, "The Rosie Crucian Secrets," Copied by Peter Smart, MA, London 1712. (Original in London Museum as Harleian Mss 6485.)

In its most subtle form, Fire is the One Only Thing, the Undivided Light, from which all is derived. Fire is energy and energy is matter. This most subtle Fire is variously called Celestial Fire, Heaven, Universal Fire, Astral Gold, Divine Will, and many more. It is described as the purest grade of fire; not burning, but gentle; invisible and known only by its operations.

It is the source of all other forms of fire and its visible representative for us is the Sun.

Remember, there is the "Sun behind the Sun," or spiritual source of which our visible star is condensed. This Celestial Fire is said to have two main aspects, the Universal and the Particular. The *Universal Fire* is diffused everywhere and excites movement in bodies. It warms and preserves the Germ of all things. It develops the Particular Fire.

The *Particular Fire* (also variously termed Innate Fire, Central Sun, or Central Fire) is implanted in each mixture with its Germ. It acts little, except when excited. It does then what the Sun, its father, does in the large universe.

This is the *Divine Spark* hidden in all things, the reflection of Celestial Fire. Called *the Quintessence*, it is the "most purified and fixed part of a matter," formed by the perfect balance of the Four Elements. This harmony between opposing forces of the Elements, brings forth a whole new and exalted state, *the Fifth Element or Quintessence*. Its action is digestive and maturing. It drives the transpiration and subtilization of the elements upward to regenerate fire.

Michael Sendivogius, in his work "The New Chymical Light" (1608) called it *The Seed:*

> "The Seed is the Elixir or Quintessence of anything, its most perfect digestion and decoction. Or again the Balm of Sulfur, which is the same as the Radical Moisture in metals."

> "The Four Elements by their continual action project a constant supply of seed to the center of the Earth, where it is digested, and whence it proceeds again in generative motions."

"This is the fountainhead of all things terrestrial."

"The Seed, which is a product of the Four Elements is projected in all directions from the Earth-center, and produces different things according to the quality of the different places."

As the Celestial Fire begins to coagulate or condense, it forms "an invisible most subtle humidity" as the Element Air. This process of *inspissation* or thickening continues and the Air condenses into the Water Element, then Water condenses into the Earth Element. The Fire trapped within (the Central Fire) now reflects and drives this process in reverse. The Earth volatilizes and becomes thickened Water. The Water volatilizes and becomes vaporous, and the Air becomes rarified into the Fire Element where it is regenerated by the Celestial Fire and the cycle begins anew.

We are talking about *occult* elements here; not the air we breathe or water we drink. This perpetual circulation of Fire is often called the *Fountain of Nature*.

"Thus Fire and Air come down into Waters and impregnate them. The Waters dispose of their thickest part and give it to the Earth. The Earth thereby becomes overloaded or saturated, which superfluity of Earth and Water is again volatilized and sublimed upwards by the Fire, (Inverted Fire or Central Fire), into vapors, which ascension and descension God has implanted into the Universal Fire as the great and only Agent of Nature"

-- "The Golden Chain of Homer"

87

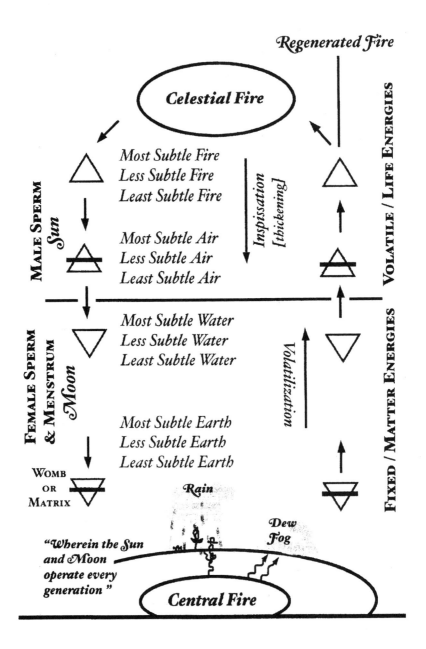

"The Earth itself is a condensed or fixed Celestial Fire and this Fire is a volatilized Earth."

-- "The Golden Chain of Homer"

This cycle of "Spiritual or Celestial Fire," in motion from the most sublime level (the Kabalistic World of Atziluth) to its most dense and concentrated form in the physical (the Kabalistic World of Assiah) then back again to the sublime, is the course of the *Active Agent* in Nature.

In the laboratory, the alchemist follows Nature in her operations; volatilizing the Earthy parts of the matter, (such as the salts and coarse oils obtained in the plant work) as well as capturing or fixing the Fire in its more ethereal forms (as in the Vegetable Mercury and volatile essential oils of the plant.) The volatile and fixed materia are united and circulated to create a new and exalted balance of the Fire inherent in the original matter.

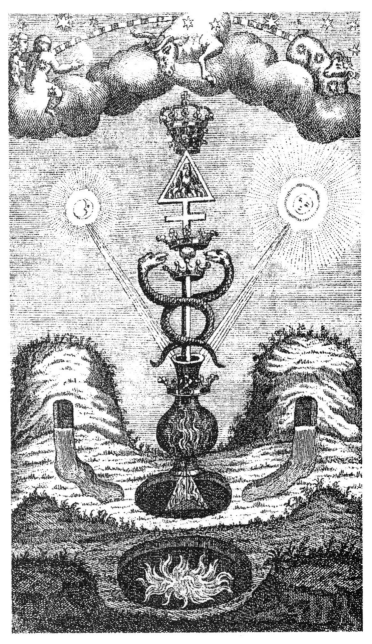

After *The Hermetical Triumph*, *1723*

Proper Medium

Modern science will agree that, in nature, energy never just disappears. It is in a constant state of transference from one form to another.

> "You can not move from one extreme to another extreme without the proper medium."

-- "The Golden Chain of Homer"

In order to move from one Elemental level to another, it is necessary to have the Proper Medium. To turn Earth into Fire you must pass through Water and Air.

One Element is the conductor of the others adjacent, and that one Element dissolves and subtilizes the other. Thus one Element is the other's magnet, solvent, volatilizing, condensing, coagulating and fixing principles.

> "Therefore if you want to unite Heaven or Fire with Earth, or convert Fire into Earth, unite it first with its nearest volatile medium and they will unite immediately. When that is done, give them Water as a medium between Air and Earth, and they will also unite; then add the Earth, and thus you may unite Fire with Earth and fix it therein; and so vice versa turn Earth into water with Water then convert it into Air, and the Air into Fire by means of Air"

-- "The Golden Chain of Homer"

This cycling of energy was often referred to as the ***Rotation of the Elements*** and forms an important key to alchemical procedure, whereby the essence of a substance is extracted, purified and raised to its most sublime state. With each rotation, the Four Elements of the matter come into greater balance and purity. When the perfect harmony is obtained, we have the *Quintessence* of the matter. The path is not so much a circle but a corkscrew, exalting the matter and drawing the Elements to a center of balance, the pinnacle of the matter.

"When thou made the quadrangle round, then is all the secret found."

Ripley 1480

CHAPTER NINE

Qabalah and Alchemy

Along this same topic we're going to introduce another concept at this juncture and talk about the Qabalah. And introduce it to your attention is all we can hope to do for, like Astrology, it is a study in itself. In fact, Alchemy, Astrology and Qabalah form the three pillars of the Hermetic Art.

> "Now, if you do not understand the use of the Qabalists and the old Astronomers, you are not born by God for the Spagyric Art, or chosen by Nature for the work of Vulcan, or created to open your mouth concerning Alchemical Arts..."

> -- Paracelsus, "Tincture of the Philosophers"

> "The Qabalah is a comprehensive approach and an integral study of all that which exists on the physical and metaphysical planes, the creation process, the ties between the created and the source of creation, the mechanisms of Nature, the various worlds and the various space-time's".

> -- Jean Dubuis (PON Lecture 1992)

The word *Qabalah* finds its root in the Hebrew word *Qibel* meaning "to receive." This receiving refers to an oral tradition of esoteric or secret knowledge concerning the mysteries of Nature. For the alchemist, Qabalah provides a symbolic representation of the path which the *One Only One* followed in the creation of the Universe (including Man) and the process of returning to Oneness along the same path.

Qabalah has always provided a means for individually approaching the spiritual dimension directly and without priestly intervention. In times past it gave a religious and philosophical freedom viewed by many as bordering on heresy. The alchemists used the symbolic framework of Qabalah as part of their secret language to both reveal and conceal certain works.

The Tree of Life

The Qabalah is presented symbolically in the form of *The Tree of Life*. The Tree contains ten centers or spheres, called the Sephiroth, which are connected by twenty two paths. Taken together, they are said to constitute the *thirty two paths of secret wisdom*. The centers are arranged in three columns. The column on the left is called the Pillar of Severity and represents the feminine aspects of the One. This column contains three Sephirah -- named *Binah* (Understanding), *Geburah* (Severity) and *Hod* (Splendor). These are related to the planetary energies of Saturn, Mars, and Mercury respectively.

The column on the right is called the Pillar of Mercy and represents the masculine aspects of the One. Contained in this column are the three Sephirah -- *Chokmah* (Wisdom), *Chesed* (Mercy) and *Netzach* (Victory). These relate to the band of the Zodiac, Jupiter, and Venus.

The middle pillar is called the Pillar of Equilibrium and represents the balance between the male and female pillars. It contains the four Sephirah -- *Kether* (Crown), *Tiphareth* (Beauty), *Yesod* (Foundation) and *Malkuth* (Kingdom).

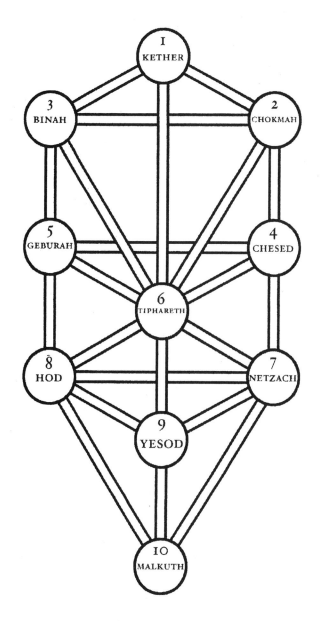

The Tree of Life

These are related to *The Undivided Light*, the Sun, the Moon, and the Earth or physical world.

One view of the Qabalah requires four of these Trees, one for each World of the Universe, stacked vertically so one tree's Malkuth gives rise to the next tree's Kether (in the same order as the Four Elements -- Fire, Air, Water, and Earth.) For ease of presentation, the four trees are usually condensed into a single tree divided into the representatives of the Four Worlds.

The Four Worlds

The Qabalah distinguishes four major planes or **Worlds of Existence** ranging from the most subtle spiritual realm to the most dense physical reality. Although it is easier to visualize and represent them as separate levels they are actually superimposed on one another and form a continuum of the One. These four worlds are briefly summarized as follows:

Atziluth: Represents the *Archetypal* world, Fire, pure Divinity, Superconsciousness, the Spiritual World, The Supernal Triad (consisting of the Spheres of Kether, Chokmah, and Binah)

Briah: Represents the *Creative* world, Air, the Archangelic, Self-consciousness, the Mental World, The Spheres of Chesed, Geburah, Tiphareth, Netzach, and Hod.

Yetzirah: Represents the *Formative* world, Water, the Angelic, Subconsciousness, the Astral World, The Sphere of Yesod

Assiah: Represents the *Material* world, Earth, man, the body, the Physical World, The Sphere of Malkuth

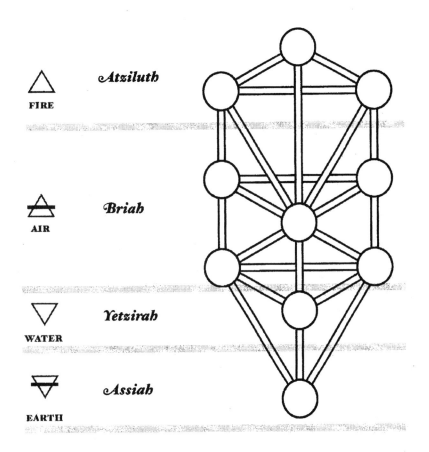

△ &Atziluth
FIRE

🜁 ᴮriah
AIR

▽ ᴚetzirah
WATER

▽ &Assiah
EARTH

The Qabalistic worldview has to do with energy and emanation. The universe issues from a single source into all we perceive -- light, matter, even space and time. The condensation of this pure energy progressively provides the illusion of matter. The study of Qabalah is a study of the Source of Energy, the areas or arena of transfer of this energy, and the behavior of this energy which is Nature. What is below is a reflection of that which is above.

Just as within the alchemical worldview, Qabalah portrays creation occurring as increasingly dense levels of energy; from the most subtle, or Fire element, to the most dense, or Earth element. Within this ocean of increasing / decreasing density, arise the Sephiroth representing unique levels of consciousness often referred to as the *spheres of being*.

Each World is a reflection of a denser or more subtle degree than the one before or after it. Each Sephirah is a reflection of the sphere which precedes it, taking on its own unique characteristics, just as the planets absorb from the Sun and radiate the excess, colored differently. Only those Spheres of The Middle Pillar have an equilibrating nature, and the ability to harmonize or reflect in total all the energies of creation.

Practical Qabalah forms a system of operation based on the interconnections and relationships revealed by the Tree of Life. Just as the planets in astrology have numerous correspondences associated with them, their interconnections and relationships are shown in the structure of the Tree. Through proper use of these correspondences it is possible to gather and direct subtle energies for alchemical work at any level of being -- progressively condensing Celestial Fire into physical manifestation.

This is where the mental and spiritual exercises of the alchemist come to bear upon the subject and finally condense into physical reality.

CHAPTER TEN

Introduction to Mineral and Metal Works

As we lead in to consideration of the work on minerals and metals, we must strongly caution you to know the theory first before attempting the praxis. The work with plants prepares us for the work with minerals, but plants are much more forgiving of mistakes and accidents. Without this developed skill, and sense of precaution based on experience, certain types of mineral work are quite deadly.

In the work with minerals and metals, we are dealing with materials in the crystalline state. They are the most dense forms of the One. The life force locked inside the crystal matrix is very pure and very powerful. We have only to look at our current technology to see the awesome power of crystalline materials, from the silicon chip to nuclear power.

Herbal elixirs are powerful tools. You could spend a lifetime exploring their possibilities; but the most powerful alchemical medicines have always been sought for in the Mineral world.

The basics of Mineral alchemy are the same as outlined in the herbal work --separation and purification of the Three Essentials followed by their reunion, and revivification. The methods are similar but tend to be longer, more complex and at higher temperatures.

As with the herbal work, the processes used in the Mineral realm work upon us in subtle ways. Because of the increased complexity of the work, you form a stronger link with your subject. Many operators have experienced the presence of *sacred space* or *a field of force* during some of the intense procedures of a mineral work.

As one of the old masters put it, "There are many paths that lead to the one effect." Likewise, we find a number of processes described for Mineral works in general as well as accomplishing *The Great Work* of confecting the Philosopher's Stone.

These processes are often broken down into two general modes: the so-called **Dry Way** and the **Wet Way**. Some masters say there is no true Dry Way as the liquid state is essential for the transference of Celestial and Vital forces in the matter.

The basic difference in the two methods of operation can be described as follows:

Via Humida -- or the **Wet Way** provokes separation of the three essentials by a process of fermentation and exaltation, or their extraction with a **Menstruum** derived from a fermentation process and determined to the particular kingdom of the matter.

Via Sicca -- or the **Dry Way**, provokes separation of the essentials by processes of calcination, fusion, sublimation, amalgamation, and dry distillation of prepared materials. The transfer of subtle principles from medium to medium occurs during fusion.

We begin our investigation into Mineral Works with practical methods used in the Via Humida or Wet Way, to extract and purify the Essentials drawn from the Mineral Realm

CHAPTER ELEVEN

Via Humida

Menstruums

In the Wet Work, the best solvent for separating the essentials is the Mercury of the particular kingdom. In the work on plants we used a Vegetable Mercury to extract or separate our three essentials. We can proceed in the same way with the Mineral and metals work by using the correct type of solvent for the work at hand.

The Alchemists called these various solvents, their *Menstruums* or *Menstrua*. These were not solvents as the modern term is generally understood. Many of them required months of preparation and, in fact, they were often prepared by following the Moon's phases. This link with the Moon partly explains the use of the term Menstruum.

They were, in addition, held to be filled with the vital life force and could transfer that Universal Fire to the subject of the operation -- even to revivify materials. Just as the menstruum nurtures and forms the fetus, so the alchemist's Menstrua possesses a nutritive power to bring forth the *Chemical Child* or *Living Medicine*.

In some texts, a special menstruum may be referred to as a *Secret Fire*, which provokes the dissolution or separation of the subject without the need of external fire.

Water, alcohol, vinegar, acetone, and ether are the most commonly used solvents in laboratory alchemy. They form the starting materials of a wide range of powerful Menstruums, useful in both Vegetable and Mineral works.

Wine and vinegar provide all the solvent power we need for Vegetable works, being the volatile and fixed spirits of that kingdom. Their combination forms the first menstruum we will be looking at, within a group of useful solvents for Mineral works.

Vegetable Radical Menstruum

The *Vegetable Radical Menstruum* is essentially a form of Liquid Vegetable Stone or *Circulatum* which properly belongs with Vegetable works, but it can be made effective to act upon minerals as well. The preparation is accomplished by the Marriage of the volatile and fixed vegetable spirits.

Ideally, we would begin with a large quantity of red wine. Half of the volume is set aside to sour and become vinegar (the Fixed Spirit). The other half is distilled to obtain the alcohol (Volatile Spirit). All of the residues that remain (the feces) are collected together in order to extract the Salt.

The wine is rectified by distillation six or seven times to obtain a strong alcohol in the usual way. The vinegar is concentrated first by freezing and later by distillation. For this you can half fill a plastic bottle with vinegar and freeze it. Take it out of the freezer and overturn it into a glass jar. After thirty minutes or so, the concentrated vinegar will have thawed and dripped into the jar
leaving a plug of ice in the plastic bottle. Discard the ice then refreeze the vinegar and repeat this thawing / freezing cycle yet a third time.

Now distill the concentrated vinegar but discard the first 1/4 to 1/3 as it is mostly water. Distill to near dryness and collect the distillate. This is the Fixed Spirit.

Combine all of the residual solids from both the wine and vinegar processing, and calcine them. Then leach out the salts and crystallize several times. Allow the salts to deliquesce for some time between crystallizations.

As the work with the salts progresses, you can blend together equal volumes of the alcohol and vinegar in a "roomy" glass vessel, seal it and allow it to circulate for a lunar cycle.

At the end of the month, add the dry and powdered salts to the cooled liquid slowly. Re-seal the container and allow this to circulate for another Lunar cycle. At the end of this second cycle, carefully distill the whole mixture to dryness.

Return the distillate to the salts that remained behind, then seal and circulate for another cycle. Repeat this cycle seven to twelve times and on the final distillation, the Menstruum will be ready. The Menstruum should completely distill and leave no residue. This liquid contains ethyl acetate *married* to the volatile plant salts and will extract the essentials from plants easily. It can be used for extracting many mineral and metal subjects such as iron and copper.

Kerkring Menstruum

The next preparation we will examine is the so called *Kerkring Menstruum* or *Philosophical Alcohol.* This preparation is attributed to the Dutch physician, Dr. Theodor Kerkring who mentions it in his commentary to Basil Valentine's "Triumphal Chariot of Antimony."

This is an example of a Vegetable spirit being *magnetized* or *determined* to activity in the Mineral realm by contact with prepared salts.

In this Menstruum, we make use of the salt ammonium chloride (NH_4Cl) or Sal Ammoniac. All of the volatile ammonium salts are valuable in alchemy and not just minerals, but plants and animals contain Sal Ammoniac. These salts sublime easily, and if not captured, will vapor away unseen.

103

The origin of Sal Ammoniac in alchemical history is hard to place. It was obtained from animal wastes for centuries, and also from the horns of horned animals, which earned it the name *Hartshorn* or *Spirit of Hartshorn*.

There is some evidence to suggest that the priests at the Temple of Amun in ancient Egypt produce it by sublimating soot. The product contained volatile ammonia salts and was called *The Salt of Amun*, then later Sal Ammoniac.

Preparation of the Menstruum begins with the sublimation of Sal Ammoniac (a commercial product is alright for this preparation). This is easily done using Corning Ware casseroles over electric or gas heat as mentioned earlier when we discussed sublimation. After the first sublimation, the sublimed crystals will take on a pale yellow color. Collect them and sublime again.

The sublimate will appear more yellow-orange and even reddish in areas. Collect and sublime a third time. After this third sublimation, the crystals will appear very yellow-orange to red-yellow and are ready for use. Store them in a glass container sealed from moisture.

Next, we need a very strong alcohol, 95% at least, and preferably from red wine.

When we have prepared these two ingredients, they are combined at the New Moon in the proportion of four parts Sal Ammoniac to ten parts Alcohol.

Seal them in a glass vessel and let digest at about 40°C for a month at least.

After digestion, the whole matter is gently distilled to near dryness. Collect the distillate and distill it again two more times. The final distillate will be the *Kerkring Menstruum*. Seal it tightly in a glass vessel for use. Collect together all of the residues from the distillations and save them as well. They can be used to *charge* more alcohol several times.

Alkahest

Alkahest is another term from Paracelsus and is used to denote not only a solvent which can extract the Sulfur and Mercury of living metals, but also one that can specifically extract the Sulfur from dead or smelted metals, and infuse them with its own vitality to reanimate them. Alkahest was thought of as a *Universal Solvent.*

Each of the Alkahests themselves possess remarkable healing power. There are a number of ways to prepare an Alkahest. We will examine two of them.

Tartar Alkahest

For the *Alkahest of Tartar*, we begin with crude tartar as it comes from the wine barrel, also called wine stone. Crush the tartar into 1/8 to 1/4 inch granules and place them into a distillation vessel. Begin distillation with a gentle heat at first then gradually increase. First a water, called the Phlegm, will come over to the receiver, then slow or stop altogether. Increase the heat and change to a new receiver with good cooling from an ice bath.

Soon the entire apparatus will fill with a thick white vapor, and a clear yellowish liquid will begin to form in the receiver, followed by drops of a black foul-smelling oil.

The distillate is now gently distilled using a water bath. The Alkahest of Tartar will come over as a clear liquid ready for use. There will also remain a nasty-smelling black oil which is the crude *Sulfur of Tartar.* This oil is reputed to have beneficial effects on diseases, involving the build up of obstructing plaques, but it must be refined by distillation before being used.

The Alkahest is effective for extraction of most of the metals, even gold and silver -- which are hard to open because of their perfect coction of the elements. This alkahest will also extract Sulfur from smelted or refined metals. In this case, the Alkahest lends its Alchemical Life to revivify the tincture and cannot be recovered for further use.

If a living mineral is extracted, the Alkahest may be recovered by gentle distillation and reused. In fact, it is said to become stronger with frequent use. The oily residue that

REAL ALCHEMY

remains behind in this distillation is dissolved into rectified wine spirits and allowed to stand. Decant the clear liquid tincture for use.

Urine, or Niter Alkahest

That's right. *Urine* -- "Held in contempt by most people, but esteemed by the wise." There are many secrets hidden in urine.

From urine we can easily obtain the volatile ammonium salts in a *Philosophical* state -- that is, alive.

Collecting the urine requires some preparation since we will only want to use the finest. A cleansing diet and restricted salt intake is undertaken for several days at least, then only water or wine during the period of collection.

Close the urine in a glass vessel and let it putrefy for a month or more in a warm place. The odors involved with this process certainly class it as an outdoor activity.

Filter the putrefied urine into a distillation train and slowly distill to dryness. Return the distillate to the solids that remain (the caput mortuum) and again digest for a month. Distill and repeat the cohobation of distillate on the solids a third time.

On the final distillation, collect the clear distillate as the *Spirit of Urine* or *Alkahest of Urine*. As this final distillation ends, you can gently increase the heat and you will see a white sublimate form in the upper glass. Collect this sublimate and save it aside for use. It is the *Volatile Salt of Urine*, also called *Van Helmont's Alkahest*. The alchemist J.B Van Helmont, a later student of the works by Paracelsus, became well known for his miracle cures using this salt.Some of this salt comes over during the distillations and is contained in the Alkahest.

This Alkahest is similar to the Kerkring Menstruum but far superior in that it is derived from live Sal Ammoniac and thus can revivify a subject. The Kerkring Menstruum cannot because we used commercial Sal Ammoniac.

"This spirit, by rectification may be made so pure and subtle that it will burn as fire and dissolve gold and precious stones."

-- French, J., "The Art of Distillation"

CHAPTER TWELVE

Concerning the Minerals

Before we continue our examination of Wet Ways, let us digress and talk about our subject matter, the products of the Mineral realm. Just as we had to gather and prepare our herbs for use, so it is with the minerals.

Depending on how we prepare our subject and the choice of menstruums, there are many useful materials derived from minerals and metals.

Preparing Ores

In the alchemical view, mineral and metal ores collected fresh from the Earth are in their natural living form and preferred to any commercial chemical substitute.

Today, people do not usually consider rocks and minerals to be alive, but to the alchemist the Mineral realm is just as full of life as the other two kingdoms of Nature. Minerals are alive. They grow, evolve, produce seed, and die just like plants and animals; but they do this at an imperceptibly slow rate.

> "The bodies of metals are domiciles of their spirits. When their terrestrial substance is by degrees made thin, extended, and purified; the life and fire hitherto lying dormant is excited and made to appear: For the life which dwells in the metals is laid hid, as it were, asleep...nor can it exert its power or show itself unless

the bodies be first dissolved and turned into their radical source. Being brought to this degree at length, by abundance of their internal light they communicate their tinging properties to other imperfect bodies."

-- "Golden Treatise of Hermes Trismegistus," quoted and footnoted in Margaret Atwood's "Hermetic Philosophy and Alchemy"

The species of the Mineral realm are just as varied as those of the Vegetable and Animal worlds. The minerals and metals appear to us in many different forms. Some of these forms are easier to find and to work with in order to provide the Essentials of each planetary type.

The Oxides, Carbonates, Sulfides and Sulfates of the metals are the most commonly preferred sources as minerals right out of the Earth.

The table below indicates some of the commonly available metal ores for each of the planets:

Planet	Common Source
Saturn	Galena, Cerrusite
Jupiter	Cassiterite
Mars	Pyrite, Magnetite
Sun	Native Gold, Placer Gold
Venus	Malachite, Azurite, Native Copper
Mercury	Cinnabar
Moon	Argentite, Cerargyrite

Plan to use five to ten pounds of raw mineral ore to begin with in general, but this is dependent on the quality of the mineral.

Take the mineral ore you have selected to work on and separate by hand as much of the *high grade* material as possible from any surrounding rock.

Fold the collected material into a piece of cloth or canvas to avoid flying debris as you strike it with a hammer. Clean out any impurities that may have been freed, then continue crushing and grinding to a fine powder. A four inch iron pipe cap fitted with a four to six inch piece of pipe makes a nice mortar for pounding ores.

Very hard stones are often heated quite hot then thrown into cold water a few times to help in reducing them to powder.

Most of the minerals have associated with them certain impurities which we want to remove. Foremost of these are the more volatile metals which may include traces of arsenic, mercury, cadmium, selenium, zinc and free sulfur. Slowly drive these off by roasting the powdered ore outside for a day or two at about 90°C. Stir the material around once in a while during the roast.

After this, you can raise the temperature slowly to about 250°C for a day to remove the last traces of arsenic. It goes without saying, that these are not things you want to be breathing, so have good ventilation.

Many ores can be extracted with a menstruum when they are in the form of the oxide. Metal oxides are called a *calx* of the particular metal. To prepare them, the powdered ore is slowly calcined at higher temperatures, ground and calcined again. The sulfide ores are often treated this way by slowly calcining the sulfur out which is replaced by oxygen to form the oxide.

Carbonate minerals are easily calcined to the oxide. They are also soluble in acidic solutions and form the salt of that acid. This offers many possibilities for purification prior to extraction by one of the prepared menstruums. Using a strong vinegar to produce the acetate of the metal is often the preferred way and this subject will be examined later.

111

The extraction of the mineral takes place much as in the Vegetable work, by covering the subject with menstruum, sealing and digesting in a warm place up to about 90°C.

After some time of digestion, and this can take months, the menstruum will take on a color or **tincture**. Filter this tincture off and gently distill the majority of the menstruum off. (Save this for future extractions.) Then allow the residue to evaporate gently down to an oily or resinous consistency.

Collect the residue and extract it into a small volume of strong alcohol. Let the alcohol extract stand for a week or two, then decant off the clear tinted liquid for use.

Some operators like to take this a step further by evaporating the alcohol extract and dissolving the residue into a small amount of ether. The ether extract is allowed to stand, decanted and evaporated. The final residue is then extracted again with alcohol and gently distilled. The distillate is collected for use and contains the most volatile essence of the metal.

This additional step helps to eliminate any metallic salts that may have carried through the extractions and so provide us with a more purified Sulfur of the metal.

Metallic Oils

"The Sulfur of the metals is an oiliness extracted from the metals themselves, endowed with very many virtues for the health of man."

-- Paracelsus

If we carefully follow the instructions of the Sages for preparing various oils and elixirs from the metals, we can indeed obtain the products they describe and this increases our confidence in their description of using the preparations.

The medicinal use of oils derived from the mineral world has a long history, with some reports bordering on the miraculous. However, as we mentioned earlier, the Vegetable world is much more forgiving of mistakes than the Mineral realm.

If one does not fully understand the theory and practice of metal works, an assumed "Tincture of Iron or Copper" may

112

just be a solution of toxic metal salts and not the true alchemical Sulfur of the metal.

Many operators consider the metal as a catalyst which acts upon the solvent to change it in characteristic ways. The actual metal is not present in the final product.

Still, the metallic works provide valuable lessons in the operations of Nature and tangible results which demonstrate the operator's progress.

There are many different oils to be obtained from the metals, depending on the subject and method of extraction. For curiosity's sake, we mention some reported effects of using metal oils medicinally and at the psychological level as summarized below. These are a selection of uses extracted from older texts, as well as reports from modern workers and thus not to be taken as medical advice.

Oil of Antimony -- Although antimony is not one of the seven ancient metals, its use in alchemy has a long history and we will be examining this in greater detail later on. Many alchemists have claimed it to be the best blood purifier available. The volatilized oil of antimony is said to help restore youth. Depending on the method of preparation, the oil of antimony rids the body of toxins by purgation, catharsis or through sweating.

There are many claims through the centuries of antimony oil curing cancer and leprosy. The Oil of Antimony is held to be nearly a universal medicine. It has a characteristic penetrating fire that will work with any other planetary medicine and deliver it powerfully to its target. Hence, it is often called the **Triumphal Chariot**.

Oil of Gold is considered to be a medicine of the highest order. It strengthens circulation as a heart tonic. It is generally strengthening to all systems and is also a good blood purifier and regenerative. It is a true universal medicine often referred to as **Potable Gold** and highly prized from ancient times.

Oil of Gold has been used successfully for treatment of rheumatism, arthritis, cancer, syphilis, uremia and multiple sclerosis. Mentally this is good for a weak will and strengthens ambition, courage, vitality and creativity.

The smallest amount of the Oil of Gold will strengthen any other herbal or mineral elixir.

Oil of Silver is effective for disorders of the brain, cerebellum, nervous system, memory, and emotions.
It is used in cases of epilepsy, depression, mania and emotional trauma. It affects the subconscious mind and dreams. It is useful in understanding one's hidden past. It helps to remove fears and mental blockages. It enhances one's psychic sensitivity and powers of imagination.

Oil of Mercury powerfully affects the nervous system, respiratory system, and liver. It is used for treating skin problems, soothing the nerves, asthma and related breathing problems. It promotes sensory awareness and quickens perceptions. It is also useful for speech problems and other troubles with communication skills.

Oil of Copper is useful for treating liver, thyroid and reproductive organ diseases. It stabilizes blood pressure and purifies the body of blood borne infections. It has been used in cases of leukemia and cancer. It enhances psychic sensitivity and attraction to the opposite sex.

Oil of Iron is another powerful regenerative for the whole body. It strengthens and purifies the blood, rapidly heals wounds, cuts, and abrasions. It is used to treat the gall bladder, pancreas, bleeding ulcers and ulcers in general. It is also said to enhance one's natural instincts. It provides an additional boost of energy, especially when mixed with Sun herbs. In fact it is said to activate the potentials of most other herbs.

Oil of Tin is useful for problems affecting the liver and lungs. It balances the way in which the body stores and uses sugars. It is held to have sudorific, vermifuge and antispasmodic properties. On the mental side, it affects the growth and wealth attitudes and brings lightheartedness to one's outlook.

Oil of Lead is especially effective for diseases affecting the bones, atrophy of the body muscular atrophy, as well as problems with the spleen. It has been used for treating acute lead toxicity, anemia, and neuropathy. It is said to increase steadiness, patience, and tolerance.

CHAPTER THIRTEEN

Via Humida: Part 2

We continue now with the methods of Via Humida, with a different and very effective Process involving the acetates of metals which we mentioned earlier.

It begins with the final menstruum we will examine for the Wet Way, which is called the *Radical Vinegar*. This liquid opens the way for obtaining the Philosophical Essentials from the mineral realm as well as one of the paths for confecting the Philosopher's Stone.

Radical Vinegar

This is a method to create a very concentrated vinegar that is loaded with Mineral Fire.

The Radical Vinegar provides a path whereby most of the Mineral and metallic realm can be opened. The starting materials are easy to find -- copper wire and red wine vinegar.

The copper wire is balled up loosely and heated to redness several times in order to oxidize it to a black color. Place the brittle mass into a glass vessel and cover with wine vinegar which has been concentrated
by freezing. Seal the container and let it digest and shake it at least daily. After some time, the liquid will become deep emerald green.

Decant the liquid into another vessel and save it aside. Repeat the process of heating the wire and extracting with fresh vinegar several times. Collect all of the liquid extracts together and filter it into a porcelain dish. Evaporate the liquid gently and collect the deep green crystals of copper acetate that form. These can be recrystallized from rainwater to further purify them.

The dry crystals are crushed, and then placed into a strong distillation apparatus.

With a cooled receiver in place, the crystals are heated first slowly, then gradually up to about 400° to 500°C. The liquid distillate is a very concentrated acetic acid and may have a slight blue-green tint. This is the Radical Vinegar. It has strength in itself to open many mineral and metallic substances, and shows its greatest utility in the preparation of metal acetates, from which we can separate the *Philosophical Mercuries* of the metals.

Philosophical Mercuries

Some alchemists refer to this as *The Acetate Path*. It stems from an Alchemical process that was a closely guarded secret for many centuries and leads to preparing *The Secret Wine Spirit of the Adepts*.

The idea behind the acetate work involves the transfer of plant life into the metal in order to accelerate its evolution.

In the general process, a mineral or metal ore is prepared as an oxide or carbonate, which is subsequently converted to an acetate using a live vinegar from wine or, even better, the Radical Vinegar.

After isolation and purification, the metal acetate is subjected to a dry distillation. That is, the crystals themselves are distilled slowly at first, then gradually increasing to about 400° to 700°C.

The products of this distillation are a volatile spirit (a *Philosophical Mercury*), an oil (the Sulfur of the metal, called the *Lion's Blood*), a watery phlegm, and a solid residue (often called the *Black Lion*) from which is obtained the Salt.

Around 1450, the English alchemist George Ripley called this distillate the **Blessed Liquor** or **Menstruum Foetens** and describes it as containing three substances:

1. The **Aqua Ardens** -- which burns like wine spirits
2. A thick white water called **Lac Virginum** or virgin's milk
3. A blood-red oil called **Sanguis Leonis** or **Blood of the Lion**

He further states that the key to all chemistry lies hidden in this **Menstruum Foetens**.

Isaac Holland describes the work on Lead Acetate, in "Opus Saturni" or "A Work of Saturn." He begins here with an already pure lead acetate – **purified Saturn**. The same method of preparation can be applied to other mineral and metal acetates:

"My Child, you may remember, that I ordered you to reserve the one half of the purified Saturn, which take and put into a Stone pot, pour upon it a bottle or more of distilled Wine Vinegar, set a head on, distill the Vinegar again from it a Bath, the head must have a hole at the top to pour fresh Vinegar upon the Matter, and abstract the Vinegar again from it, pour fresh Vinegar again on, and again abstract it; this pouring on, and abstracting or distilling off must continue so long, till the Vinegar be drawn off as strong as it was when it was put in, then is it enough, and the Matter hath in it as much of the Spirit of Vinegar as it can contain; then take the Pot out of the Bath, take off the head, and take the Matter out, and put it into a thick glass which can endure the Fire, set a head on it, put it in a Cupel with Ashes, which set on a Furnace, first make a small Fire, and so continually a little stronger, till your Matter come over as red as Blood, thick as Oil, and sweet as Sugar, with a Celestial Scent, then keep it in that heat so long as it distills, and when it begins to slack, then increase your Fire till the Glass begins to glow,

119

continue this heat till no more will distill, then let it cool of itself, take the Receiver off, stop it very close with Wax, take the Matter out of the Glass, beat it to powder in an Iron Mortar, with a steel Pestle; and then grind it on a Stone with good distilled Vinegar, put this Matter so ground into a Pot, pour good distilled Vinegar upon it, that two parts be full, set the Pot into a Bath with a head upon it, distill the Vinegar off, pour fresh Vinegar again upon it, distill it off again: thus do so long, that the Vinegar be as strong as it was when it was first poured upon it, then let it cool, take the Matter out of the Bath, take the head off, take the Matter out of the Pot, put it into a stronger round Glass which can endure the Fire, as you did before, set it upon a Furnace in a Cupel with sifted Ashes, set a head, and a Receiver luted to it, then distill it, first with a small fire, which augment by degrees, till a Matter come over red as Blood, and thick as Oil, as aforesaid; give it fire till no more will distill, then let it cool of itself, take off the head, break the glass pot, and take the Matter out, powder it again, and grind it on a Stone with distilled Vinegar, put it again into the Stone pot, pour fresh Vinegar upon it, set it into the Bath, and its' head on, distill the Vinegar from it, pour it on again as hath been taught, till the Vinegar remain strong as it was.

Reiterate this distillation in the Bath until the Matter hath no more Spirit of the Vinegar in it, then take it out, set it in a glass pot, distill all that will distill forth in ashes, till the Matter become a red Oil, then have you the most noble Water of Paradise, to pour upon all fixed stones, to perfect the Stone; this is one way. This water of Paradise thus distilled, the Ancients called their sharp, clear Vinegar, for they conceal its name."

The metal or mineral ore we have selected to work on is converted into its acetate form and distilled in this crystalline state. During this distillation, as the temperature is rising, moisture will begin to collect and come over into the recipient. This is mostly water that was associated within the crystalline acetate -- the so-called *water of crystallization*. Collect this water and save it aside. This is called the *Phlegm*, and is used to extract the salts later. As the heat increases, the phlegm will stop distilling over. Attach a fresh receiver and continue heating. Soon you will see a thick, heavy, white vapor coming over and a golden liquid form in the receiver, which must be kept very cold or this spirit will escape. The final distillation temperature may be in the range of 400° to 700°C, and by this time you will notice drops of blood-red oil distilling over, the apparatus being filled with dense white vapor so as to appear made of chalk. Let the apparatus cool and save the distillate tightly sealed. This liquid appears red like wine and called the *Menstruum Foetens* or *Secret Wine Spirit*.

Gentle distillation of this liquid will yield a clear, very volatile liquid containing the *Philosophical Mercury* of the metal and a deep red liquid which contains the *Philosophical Sulfur* of the metal. These are called the *Red and White Wine*.

The volatile liquid or *Philosophical Mercury* is purified by distillation several times. This liquid contains mostly acetone with some of the more volatile components of the oil. In fact, this was the way acetone was made industrially until the early 1900s, by which time its alchemical roots had largely been forgotten. This was becoming evident even by the 1850s, when a medical doctor named C.A. Becker investigated this preparation. Becker presents case histories for the successful treatment of flu, nervous complaints, rheumatism, headaches, fevers and paralysis using the volatile spirit, which he termed *Spiritus Aceti Oleosus* because it was prepared in the old way and still contained some of the volatile oils, unlike the commercial product. Becker considered these *etheric oils* to be essential to the medical effects and urged his fellow physicians to regain possession of this valuable remedy.

The red liquid or *red wine* is also purified by gentle distillation. First, a clear acidic phlegm will come over. The thick blood-red oil that remains can be distilled at a higher temperature or often it is just dissolved in alcohol and the clear tinted liquid is decanted for use. These oils are analogous to the essential oils obtained from plants and their chemical composition is just as complex. The solid residue from the acetate distillation is generally removed and calcined, then extracted with the combined phlegm and crystallized to obtain the Salt.

The distillation residue from lead is interesting as it is mostly composed of fine particles of lead metal and will rapidly oxidize on exposure to the air. Very often it will ignite on its own and become like a red hot coal, burning itself to ashes.

Any pure salt of the particular metal can be used as the body; even a "dead" commercial salt, which is then reanimated with the Mercury and Sulfur as we did in the Vegetable work.

Holland describes an operation along these lines which requires thirty to thirty two weeks to produce a solid medicine or *Stone* from lead, of which he says:

> "My child, there are some people who have external distempers on their bodies such as fistulas, cancer, wolf, or evil biles or holes, be they what or how they will, etc. Give such a one the weight of one wheat corn to drink in warm wine two days as is taught before. The whole body will, within and without, be freed from all which is adverse to nature."

> "And if the party will take the like quantity of a wheat corn every day for the space of nine days, I tell you, his body will be as spiritual as if he had been nine days in the terrestrial paradise eating every day of the fruit, making him fair, lusty, and young. Therefore, use this stone weekly, the quantity of a wheat corn with warm

wine, so shall you live in health until your last hour of the time appointed for you by God."

This illustration from "The Art of Distillation" shows the basic design for the acetate work. The still pot on the furnace holds the acetate, then the vapor is led through a cooling system into a receiver. This will catch the bulk of the distillate. A cooling system, using a barrel of ice water, leads off from this receiver to a second receiver which catches the more volatile spirits.

Some artists make the distinction that Philosophical Mercuries are derived from the metals; while the minerals produce an Alkahest.

CHAPTER FOURTEEN

Via Sicca

The *Dry Way* of working is held to be faster, but at greater danger and requiring some developed skills. Many of these works require fierce heat, toxic materials, and molten salts or metals as well as some agility in manipulating them.

There are some artists who eschew the violent methods of the Dry Way with its high fusion temperatures and corrosive salt mixtures.

"Fire is the life of metals while they are still in their ore, and the fire of smelting is their death," says Sendivogius.

The death of the material, its **putrefaction**, is the key that releases the spiritual components from the prison of the body. The trick in either the Wet or Dry Way is to be able to capture the subtle essence into a suitable vehicle before they can vapor away.

> "To grasp the invisible elements, to attract them by their material correspondences, to control, purify and transform them by the living power of the spirit, this is true alchemy."
>
> -- Paracelsus

In the solid state, the body is subjected to the forces of Earth and the Universal Fire is held prisoner within the body.

The methods of the Dry Way create an open entrance to the bodies of minerals and metals to release their trapped Quintessence.

Most of these operations involve either amalgamation with metallic mercury, melting or fusion of the materials; since the vital and spiritual energies transfer in the liquid state but they will escape if not captured by a *magnet* or proper medium.

The Hand of the Philosophers

The alchemical Sulfur and Mercury are released and captured by "The Hand of the Philosophers:"

In laboratory alchemy, there are a handful of mineral salts which are of great utility in *unlocking* mineral and metallic essences. Isaac Holland called them *The Hand of the Philosophers*. These five salts act as *Keys* to open materials. They can be combined and prepared in many different ways in order to unlock any metal or mineral so that its spiritual essence is available for extraction by a suitable medium.

"In the power of the salts and their preparation lies the whole art of alchemy."

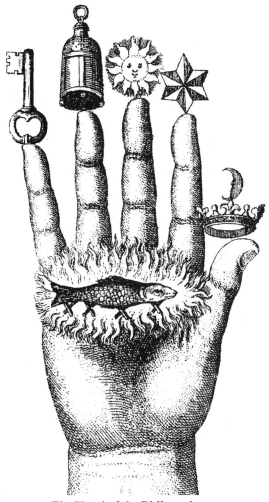

The Hand of the Philosophers

127

Niter

The first and foremost salt placed on the Hand is Niter or Saltpeter, which Holland calls the *King of Salts* and the *Crown*. It is the thumb of the hand.

"He is the mill, through which everything must be ground". Today we call it potassium nitrate (KNO_3) and it is a powerful oxidizer -- the main ingredient in gunpowder.

In the old days, niter was obtained from specially prepared and attended piles of decomposing plant and animal wastes, wood ashes, and loose soil. The nitrogen-containing compounds decompose and form nitric acid which reacts with the potassium salts in the plant ash to form potassium nitrate. This all takes some time, at least one to three years, so there would be many different *niter beds* working to harvest at any time.

At harvest, the pile is leached with water and the water evaporated to obtain the niter as crystals which are then purified by recrystallizing several times.

The commercial potassium nitrate of today is usually generated from the waste products of other chemical processing industries and is not considered to be *Philosophical*.

This holds true for most of these salts we are discussing. Prior to use they must be *reanimated* or recharged with Fire.

In the case of niter, it should be recrystallized from rainwater several times, allowing it to absorb the moisture of the air in between crystallizations, at the very least. An even better trick is to recrystallize the commercial product after solution in fresh urine followed by crystallization from rainwater.

> "Niter is the corporified spirit of the stars, and therein is the nature of metals. Niter is the body of the stars, whose central fire or Sulfur is called Sol."
>
> -- LaFontain, F., "Curious Aphorisms Concerning the Universal Salt of Nature," 1797.

Vitriol

Depicted as the index finger of the Hand and a six pointed star, is Vitriol.

Today this term usually denotes the blue crystalline salt, copper sulfate; or the green crystals of iron sulfate, but there are other vitriols as well. There are writings describing the use of these materials dating to at least 600 B.C.E.

This mineral is found near deposits of sulfide ores such as Pyrite, where water leaches it out of the weathering ore. Some of the old texts refer to this salt as *Atrament*, recalling its use as a blackening agent for inks and leather while other texts refer to it as *Lixivium of Marcasites* in reference to how it is prepared. (Marcasites are the sulfide ores.)

The vitriols are easily soluble in water so their purification by recrystallization is easy.

You can produce your own vitriol though it takes some time. Collect together ten to twenty pounds (at least) of iron pyrite (FeS) and grind it to powder. Spread the powder out onto a large flat iron tray then alternately roast it gently and spray with rainwater to moisten, then dry.

Repeat this process of artificially weathering the ore many times over the course of several months. Now place the *weathered* ore into a container and wash it well with rain water. Save all of the wash water together and continue weathering the ore that remains.

Decant or filter the wash water into a wide bowl and allow it to evaporate. A few drops of concentrated sulfuric acid may be added to retard air oxidation of the solution. You will soon see beautiful emerald green crystals forming which you will collect and keep in an air tight container.

These green crystals can be purified by recrystallization from rain water into very glassy, transparent crystals of ferrous sulfate ($FeSO_4 - 7H_2O$). In fact, the name vitriol derives from the Latin *vitrum*, meaning glass.

Many of the ancient authors sing praises to the utility of vitriol. Basil Valentine called it *The True Mineral Salt* which contains the Red and the White spirits.

129

If vitriol alone is distilled, there will first come over a clear liquid (the White spirit) with a strong sulfur dioxide odor. Keep this tightly sealed and the choking odor will disappear as the dissolved sulfur dioxide oxidizes to form a mild solution of sulfuric acid.

As the heat is increased quite high, there will finally ascend a more viscous, reddish liquid which is a concentrated sulfuric acid filled with martial essence (the Red spirit).

Sal Ammoniac

We briefly met this salt in the preparation of Kerkring Menstruum. Sal Ammoniac is the Star of the Hand at the middle finger.

"The Spirit of all things is Sal Ammoniac."

"Sal Ammoniac can unite all things that are antagonistic and cannot be mixed so that afterwards they mix and conjugate."

-- Isaac Holland, "Opera Vegetabilis"

The amazing thing about this salt is its ability to sublimate easily and in doing so, it changes from the solid state directly into vapors of hydrochloric acid and ammonia only to reunite on a cool surface as the solid salt again. It is this extremely corrosive atmosphere that serves to open many of the metals for extraction.

When mineral or metal ores are mixed with Sal Ammoniac and sublimated, their more subtle parts are caught up in this vapor and deposited with the sublimate, purified and opened up.

To illustrate, here is a method for preparing a tincture from silver as given by the twentieth century alchemist Fulcanelli:

To begin, we need **Horn Silver** which occurs as the mineral Cerargyrite, consisting mainly of silver chloride. Pure silver metal dissolved into nitric acid then precipitated with a solution of sea salt will also work for this experiment. Wash the precipitate (which is silver chloride) with water then dry it. Next, mix it with three times its weight of Sal Ammoniac and grind it well together.

Now gently sublime the powder and collect all that will come over. Dissolve the sublimate in rainwater and let it settle. You will see a red to brown fine solid fall to the bottom. This solid contains the Lunar Sulfur. Decant off the clear liquid and save it. Wash the solids several times with rainwater then place the solids into a dish to dry. Collect together all of the dried solid as a powder then extract it with rectified wine alcohol (95% or better) for a month. The resulting clear, golden alcohol extract is a *Tincture of Silver* and contains the Lunar Sulfur for use.

Your Sal Ammoniac can be recovered for future use by evaporating the liquid you decanted from the solids earlier.

Alum

The Lantern of the Hand at the ring finger is Alum. Properly speaking, Alum is a vitriol being the double sulfate of potassium and aluminum $KAL(SO_4)_2$, but has been such a versatile mineral since ancient times that its in a class of its own. It has been used for cleaning and deodorizing, as a mordant for dyes, to prepare leather, and as an astringent and styptic to close wounds.

Alum has a low melting point ($92.5°C$) and so it is often added to assist fusion of other salts and mineral bodies. At higher temperatures Alum releases sulfur oxides in large amounts and so assists the production of sulfuric acid.

Being soluble in water, Alum is easily purified for use by recrystallization.

The best native source for this is the mineral Alunite (or Alum stone), which is ground and roasted, then dissolved in water. After filtration, the water is evaporated to obtain crystals of Alum.

Salt

The Key of the Hand, on the little finger is salt. This is common salt, sodium chloride (NaCl), obtained as sea salt or that which is mined from the earth, called *Sal Gemma*.

The Fixed Spirit of Salt

Salt itself has great healing power when rightly prepared. Such a preparation is the *Fixed Spirit of Salt* as given by Holland.

Take sea salt and grind it fine in a mortar, then dissolve it into distilled vinegar from white wine. Filter the solution into a wide bowl and gently heat to evaporate the liquid.

Soon a crust or skin will begin to form at the surface of the liquid. Collect this carefully with a skimmer and save it aside. Holland calls this the *Spiritus* of the salt. Continue collecting this as it forms until the liquid volume is too small. Take all the remains and repeat the solution with vinegar, evaporation and collection of the Spiritus a second time. Collect all of the Spiritus together and save for use. It is not Fixed at this stage.

The residue that remains in the bowl is called the *Corpora* of the salt. This same purification can be used for other salts as well. Holland says:

> "One cannot work with any salt unless the spiritus has first been separated from the corpus. As you separate the spiritus from the corpora of common salt, thus is also separated the spiritus from the corpora of all other things."

To fix the Spiritus of salt, we must first recrystallize it from rainwater several times.

Dry the crystals, powder them in a mortar, then add Sal Ammoniac at about 1/10th the total weight of salt. Seal this in a tall flask and allow it to digest for at least a month.

Take out the salt and gently dry, then seal in a glass container for use. This is the Fixed *Spiritus Salis* which is said to have miraculous healing virtues.

Dissolving Waters and Mineral Acids

One common use of these various salts is the preparation of *Aqua Fortis* or *Strong Waters*.

Combinations of salts are distilled at high temperatures to produce the mineral acids such as sulfuric, nitric and hydrochloric acids. The resulting Strong Water is used for the preparation and purification of mineral bodies.

For example, we can combine equal parts of niter and vitriol and add 1/3 part of Alum, then distill up to about 800°C. This will yield (about 20% by weight of the solids) a solution of nitric acid with a concentration around 50% $HNO3$.

Vitriol can be distilled alone or with Alum to produce sulfuric acid. Concentrated sulfuric acid will react with common salt to produce hydrochloric acid.

Aqua Regia is the *King's Water*, so-called because it is strong enough to dissolve gold -- the King of Metals. It is commonly made by mixing three parts hydrochloric acid with one part nitric acid, but in the old days it had to prepared by mixing and distilling salts. For example, we can mix two parts niter with one part Sal Ammoniac and distill at a high temperature to form Aqua Regia.

Another recipe is to mix four parts vitriol, six parts niter and one part Alum, then distill them. Add Sal Ammoniac to the distillate and it will dissolve gold, silver, and sulfur.

Salts can also be combined in dry form with many materials and effect their dissolution. The reactions generally take longer and thus are not as violent as the concentrated mineral acids.

For example, the mixing of niter and sal ammoniac as powders, to which is added a metal to be dissolved. A few drops of rain water will help get the reaction going. This mixture will generate Aqua Regia slowly and dissolve the metal. Not all of the reaction mixtures are slow so try a small amount first. One spectacular example of this is the mixture of four parts Sal Ammoniac, one part Dew Salt, and four parts powdered zinc. A few drops of water placed on top of a small pile of the powder begins a reaction that shortly causes the material to burst into flame.

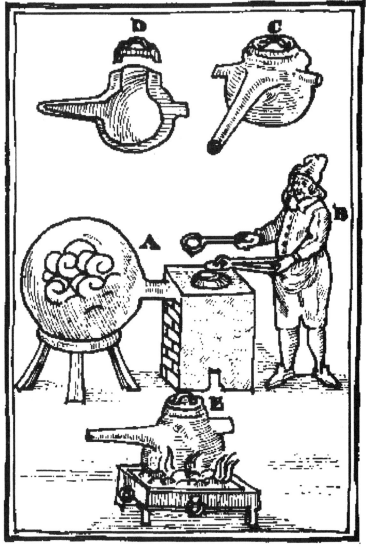

From *The Art of Distillation*

The illustration above depicts an apparatus useful for the distillation of "Strong Waters" by adding spoonfuls of salts slowly.

Dry Menstruum

Salts are used in Dry methods as *Dry Menstrua*. Just as the liquid menstrua of the Wet Way extract and retain the essentials in Vegetable and Mineral works, the Dry Way achieves the state of total liquefaction of the mineral or metal by high temperature fusion aided by select salts. Much of this technology stems from the very ancient arts of glassmaking and ceramics.

Salts in addition to those of the Hand include our old friend Salt of Tartar, and the related sodium carbonate or Natron; both used extensively in glass and ceramic glazes for their relative ease of fusion (about 900°C) and ability to dissolve many mineral bodies. These are often referred to as the Alkali Carbonates or just Alkali.

The Fixed Salt of Tartar (K_2CO_3) is said to "penetrate every metal on fusion and takes from them the Sulfurous part." Alchemist George Starkey in his work "The Art of Volatilizing Alkalis" speaks of the process wherein the "Calx of an imperfect metal" is fused with Alkali in order to extract its Sulfur.

If you have some experience with the Ens tincture process described earlier, this operation has similarities but is adapted to mineral and metal bodies.

We mentioned the corrosive nature of Tartar Salt and the deliquescence liquid. This corrosiveness is greatly intensified in the fused salt, giving it the power to liquefy minerals and metals rapidly.

Begin by heating a large porcelain crucible and fusing the Salt of Tartar until it is about half full. When it is molten, slowly add your powdered ore (generally in the form of an oxide but not always) and allow it to fuse. Stir occasionally with an iron rod.

Continue adding portions of the ore and additional Tartar Salt to maintain complete flux of the matter. Now we have two options, let the contents cool in the crucible and break it out

135

later or cast the molten liquid out onto a smooth heat-resistant surface.

Collect the solidified matter and grind it while it is still warm. Again we have a few options: one -- allow the powdered mass to deliquesce; then extract the metal's Sulfur with Kerkring Menstruum just as in the Ens tincture process. The second way is to dissolve the mass into rainwater and allow the solids to settle. The solids are collected and dried, then extracted with a prepared menstruum.

The final extract will contain the Sulfur of the metal and if an Alkahest was used in the extraction, it will also be reanimated with fresh Fire.

This operation is a little Wet and Dry but helps to illustrate some of the possibilities of methods involved.

YSOPAICA

Another valuable process which is somewhat obscure is called **Ysopaica** -- the art of washing things white by fire. It does not really fit in as a specifically wet or dry method and is more an auxiliary method of purifying extracts from plant or mineral sources.

Paracelsus mentions this process in his writings, and Rudolf Glauber, who was a later follower of the works of Paracelsus praised it greatly.

The roots of Ysopaica go back to the burnt offerings of the ancient temples, the idea being that the most purified essence of a material is driven off to the heavens by the action of fire.Frater Albertus often said "that which is essential is not destroyed by the fire, it is only purified thereby."

Glauber, in his work "De Purgatorio Philosophorum" (circa 1650), writes:

> "The flame of fire can consume nothing but its like ie, the combustible sulfur, but cannot consume the incombustible mercury, nor destroy, burn or annihilate it, the flames only serving to meliorate and exalt it. For the mercury of all things can no way better be purged

than by fire, by which though it be driven away, yet may always be found again, as being incombustible."

"Vegetables, animals, and minerals with the help of any burning spirit, not only that of wine, but of corn, honey, fruits, leaves or grass, may be most highly purified and reduced to the highest medicines."

The practice is fairly simple and basically consists of obtaining an alcoholic extract from Vegetable, Animal or Mineral subjects, and igniting the alcohol under a cooling dome or similar cooling setup that will capture the hot vapors that arise and then condensing them.

"This spirit of wine being kindled burns away and the mercury of the most pure essential salt is thereby loosened and with the flame goes over into the receiver where it is caught of the phlegm from which being separated by distillation in a vaporous bath it is fit for use."

As a simple example, we can take red wine and distill out the alcohol which is then rectified several times. The remaining wine liquid is evaporated to a thick honey-like residue. This honey is then distilled at a higher temperature to obtain a black stinking oil which contains healing virtue locked inside its impure and stinking form.

This black oil is dissolved in the rectified wine spirit, then ignited under the cooling helm where the hot vapors will be condensed. The resulting distillate can be used as is or subjected to a gentle distillation to obtain a small amount of volatile solid which Glauber calls the *incombustible mercury* of the subject and a powerful medicine.

"This method of using the burning spirit works on all stinking, impure, vegetable, animal, and easily inflammable mineral subjects, whereby they are washed to the highest degree of purity, with which great things may be performed."

137

In the work with minerals and metals, the subject is treated with salts as mentioned above, extracted with one of the menstruums, such as Kerkring Menstruum, and the resulting extract is burned under a cooling helm. The resulting distillate is used as is or the gentle distillation to obtain a volatile salt completes the preparation.

> "In the same way we can extract tinctures from iron, copper, antimony, and sulfur, and with the assistance of the flame of spirit of wine, maturate them into most lovely, fragrant, incombustible tinctures.For by means of our microcosmical salt, all metals and minerals may be reduced to potability, without the help of corrosive, in which state they are the most powerful medicaments imaginable."

The yields from this method tend to be small but very powerful in effect.

> "Learn to prepare medicines by fire; because whatsoever can without hurt or loss abide the fire, the same must needs be pure and good."

> "The art of washing things snow white by philosophical purgatory fire appears to be the head skill of philosophy, physik, and alchemy."

> -- Glauber, "De Purgatorio Philosophorum"

Frontispiece to *The Triumphal Chariot of Antimony* **by Basil Valentine**

CHAPTER FIFTEEN

Antimony

It is often said that once you begin on the alchemical path, strange things happen in the form of coincidence (or synchronicity) to attract toward yourself information and materials that are required for your continued journey.

This certainly was the case for me and antimony. I had just returned from the PRS class centered on the wonders of antimony and was anxious to start the work. Within a month, and by an odd series of events, I found myself working underground in an antimony mine I did not know existed, only sixteen miles from my home. Needless to say, I soon found myself in possession of all the *fresh picked* antimony required for many experiments.

Antimony has always held a special place in alchemy. Known from very ancient times, other names for Antimony are Mestem, Asinat, Stimmi and Stibium from which we get our symbol for the element Sb. Antimony is considered a toxic metal, very similar to arsenic. The fascination with this material led to abuse and scams which caused the death of many who had heard of its healing virtues. This provoked Parliament in 1566 to forbid its use in medicine for about one hundred years.

Antimony is said to be the mineral of Malkuth. Earth is its planetary ruler. It contains the rays of all the other planets, and because of this is said to be immortal. Its spirit is fixed to the sphere of Earth.

> "The ancients knew about antimony, praising it very highly for its hidden medicinal virtues. During medieval times, a rediscovery of these virtues by Basil Valentine and the "father" of modern medicine, Paracelsus, caused considerable renewed interest. Both found antimony to be of extraordinary curative potency and wrote extensively about it. Valentine called antimony one of the Seven Wonders of the World, praising it as the best blood-purifying agent available. He claimed to have used it for the cure of many diseases, including cancer. These claims were substantiated by Dr. Kerkring of Holland about two hundred and fifty years later when he prepared and used antimonial tinctures in his medical practice."

> -- Frater Albertus

There is a great power hidden in antimony which is often depicted in alchemical images as a black dragon, a venomous serpent, a wolf, or an orb surmounted by a cross.

The authoritative text on the many preparations of antimony is Basil Valentine's "The Triumphal Chariot of Antimony" which first appeared around 1600, though others argue that it is two hundred to three hundred years older.

ANTIMONY ORES

By far the most common source of antimony is the sulfide ore called Stibnite ($Sb_2 S_3$) or antimony trisulfide. When the old texts speak of antimony, they are generally referring to this sulfide ore, and when speaking of metallic antimony, they designate it as *Regulus* or *Little King*.

141

Stibnite very often has impurities of arsenic, mercury, bismuth, lead, and uncombined sulfur, so it is common practice to roast the ore prior to use in order to eliminate these as much as possible. Begin this roasting gently at about 90°C for a day, then slowly increase to about 250°C.

Some consider that these common impurities earned the mineral the name *Anti Monos* or *not alone*, from which we get our modern word Antimony.

A long slow calcination will eliminate all of the sulfur and produce a very light gray to white antimony oxide suitable for many works. This calcination is at a much higher temperature than roasting, but keep it below 520°C or melting will begin at the start. Later, as the sulfur vaporizes and the ore looks lighter, the temperature can be increased. Stir the powder around with an iron rod once in a while to assist the oxidation. Antimony oxide is somewhat volatile at these temperatures, so be sure not to overdo the time and temperature. This is outside work or to be done under a fume hood.

Kermes Mineral

One of the strange properties of antimony is that it acts as an acid or an alkaline material depending on its environment. They call this being *amphoteric*.

By taking advantage of this property, it is possible to purify Stibnite, even low grade ores, with a chemical process. The result of this purification is a red-brown powder called *Kermes*, named after a dye of this color made from insects.
Chemically it is known as antimony oxysulfide.

The preparation is easy but involves some foul smelling odor like rotten eggs, so again this is outside work or in a fume hood.

Start by grinding the ore to a fine powder. Then set it aside until we need it. Now prepare a strong alkali solution by dissolving Lye (sodium hydroxide) into rainwater. A 20 to 30% solution works well. This will get very hot as the lye dissolves, so add it slowly to avoid boiling. Also wear eye and hand protection.

Start adding the powdered stibnite to the still hot lye solution while stirring with a non-metal rod. The amount of ore added depends on its quality, but it is better to add it in excess to the weight of lye used. We can do this alkaline leaching several times to pull out all of the antimony. The solution can even be heated to near boiling to hasten the dissolution of the stibnite.

After an hour of digestion, let the solution settle a bit, then filter it through a wad of glass wool. This solution is very caustic and will eat right through paper filters. You can find glass wool at aquarium suppliers.

The resulting solution will be of a deep golden yellow color. Into this solution, slowly pour in a 10 to 30% solution of acetic acid until the solution pH is seven or neutral.

This is the smelly part mentioned earlier. A lot of hydrogen sulfide is released which is quite toxic, so definitely be outside and upwind.

As the acetic acid is added you will begin to see a red-brown solid form and fall to the bottom. This is the *Kermes Mineral*.

Allow the solids to settle, then decant the clear liquid from the top and save it aside. This liquid contains mostly sodium acetate which can be recovered for use in the acetate work. Its previous association with antimony makes it even more valuable.

The still moist Kermes is washed several times with rainwater by covering it with ten to twenty times its volume of water and letting it settle, then decant and repeat. Place the wet solid into a dish to dry.

The resulting red-brown powder, the Kermes, is now cleansed of many impurities that are associated with antimony ores including the alumina and silica matrix. Chemically, the powder represents a complex mixture of antimony trisulfide and antimony trioxide.

Other alkalis will also work to dissolve the stibnite, such as potassium hydroxide, salt of tartar, even liquid ammonia. By altering the concentrations, and order of mixing the acid and alkali solutions, the powder can be made to take on shades of canary yellow to brilliant orange to crimson red as the particle size varies.

143

Kermes is much easier to calcine to a light oxide powder because of its greater purity.

Glass of Antimony

Another property of antimony is that it is a glass-former. Ancient glass and ceramic artifacts bear witness to this knowledge far back in time.

Preparation of the glass begins with the calcination of stibnite or Kermes into the oxide. This conversion to the oxide need not be too rigorous as a small proportion of the sulfide is needed to help form the glass. If you melt pure antimony oxide you will see a beautiful orange liquid, but when it is cast and cooled it will revert to an opaque yellowish-white crystalline mass. The presence of antimony sulfide mixed into the antimony oxide will promote the formation of transparent glasses of intense red, yellow and orange shades. The finely ground antimony oxide / sulfide is fused in a strong porcelain crucible at a temperature of about 700° to1000°C, sometimes even up to 1300°C. It helps to add a small amount of the raw stibnite powder in doing this to obtain a deep ruby red glass. Some use borax as a flux, but this often leads to problems in removing it later. In fact, some claim that borax as well as aluminum lead to alchemical death of the subject and avoid their use at all costs.

When the crucible is 3/4 full, and entirely molten, stick a thin iron rod into it and pull it out. Look at the glass adhering to the rod, if it is transparent then it is ready. If it is cloudy, continue heating until it clarifies. However, do not overdo the fusion for too long as the material will be volatilizing throughout the process.

When the melt is ready, use tongs and quickly pour the liquid out into a wide flat dish of copper. Once cool, you will have the glass of antimony. It should be transparent and generally of a yellow to deep red tint, although by altering proportions and heating it is possible to obtain glasses of other colors, even green and blue. The glass is held by many to be the preferred starting material for extracting the Sulfur of antimony.

Prior to extraction with one of the prepared menstruums, the glass must be ground to a very fine powder.

Vinegar of antimony

Stibnite is one of the few minerals that seem to undergo fermentation similar to making wine, but at higher temperatures. The resulting liquid is known as the *Vinegar of Antimony* or the pure *Fixed Spirit of Antimony*, and is nearly a Universal Menstruum for the Mineral world as well as a powerful medicine for internal and external use.

Begin by grinding several pounds of Stibnite to a fine powder. Roast the powder at about 90°C for a day to remove arsenic, mercury, and any free sulfur that may be present. After cooling the ore, mix three parts of it with seven parts of distilled rainwater by weight. Seal in a flask and digest at 40° to 50°C, shaking it frequently. This is the part that takes some time. Up to a year or longer is often allowed for the fermentation to occur.

As the Antimony Spirit enters the water you may perceive the liquid to be more viscous and soapy or foamy. This is a good sign the ore has opened. Now the flask of material is attached to a distillation train. Begin the distillation slowly at 80°C and slowly raise it to about 400°C over a period of three days.

Let the apparatus cool completely. You should see a yellow to red sublimate on the walls of the glassware, or as a crust above the stibnite residue. Return the distillate to the residue, rinsing all of the sublimate from the walls. Repeat this distillation cycle two more times. The liquid from the final distillation is the Vinegar of Antimony.

In this form it is still a weak solution but has excellent healing qualities of its own. Basil says it will eliminate all toxins from the body.

We can concentrate this Fixed Spirit through distillation such that it will extract the Sulfur from gold in a short time. The best way to approach this is by a 4x3 distillation to obtain twelve fractions. This separation opens other possibilities for medicinal use but our interest now is in concentrating the Vinegar. The name "vinegar" is applied to this liquid because of its fermentive origin and its acidic nature, and though it is not acetic acid nor sulfuric acid, the concentrate can reach a pH of one. Test the pH of each of the twelve fractions and combine those which are most acidic.

Distill this combined liquid into four equal parts and test the pH. Continue the process of distillation, testing, and combining until you have isolated the distillate with a pH of one. This is the concentrated Vinegar of Antimony. The yield is generally small but very powerful medicinally and as a menstruum it will extract the essentials from virtually all of the Mineral realm.

Oil of Antimony

There are many ways to obtain an oil from antimony, and the properties of these oils vary with their method of preparation.

One of the most important and valuable of these is the *Fixed Red Oil*.

The preparation begins with the calcination of stibnite or Kermes into the oxide form. The oxide is ground very fine and made into glass of antimony. This glass is powdered and then extracted with a strong solution of vinegar, or still better, with radical vinegar. Let the extraction continue for several weeks at about 40°C and agitate it once in a while, especially in the first few days, or it will coalesce into a thick mass. After this time the solution will take on a golden to deep red color. Filter off the extract, and repeat with fresh vinegar.

Combine all of the extract and filter it into a distillation vessel. Gently distill the liquid until it becomes thickened, then add some water to dissolve the residue and continue the distillation.

146

Repeat this washing with water to remove as much of the acid as possible. This washing can also be performed using alcohol. In this case, ethyl acetate is formed and readily distills out, so the washing is faster.

The resulting residue will appear as a golden brown, gummy resin.

Place the resin into a suitably sized distillation vessel and proceed to distill as in the acetate work. Drops of a blood-red oil will come over, which are carefully collected by dissolving them into alcohol. Rinse any of the oil adhering to the glassware out with alcohol and combine all of the liquid into a container. Seal and allow it to stand for several days, then decant the clear tinted extract for use. This *Fixed Tincture of Antimony* has powerful healing properties unrecognized by modern medicine.

Star Regulus

The final preparation of antimony we will briefly examine is that of the so-called *Star Regulus of Antimony*.

This preparation is considered to be an advanced alchemical work as there is some danger involved and requires the operator to have developed laboratory skills. Many of the ancient sages describe this operation in extremely veiled terms.

Some of the clearest writings come from such notables as Eiraneus Philalethes, Nicholas Flamel, and even Isaac Newton. In fact, this path is often referred to as *The Flamel Path*. Taken to completion, it leads to the confection of The Philosopher's Stone and as such, represents the summit of laboratory alchemical works in the Dry Way.

The term *Regulus of Antimony* has always been used to refer to the metallic antimony reduced from its ore. When it is well prepared and purified, you will see a starry pattern on the surface of the metal. The metal itself is quite brittle and reduces to a powder fairly easily. Hidden in the Regulus is the spirit of antimony.

"In Antimony are Mercury (in the regulus), Sulfur (in the redness) and Salt (in the black earth which sinks to the bottom), which three, corrected, separated, and finally united together in the proper manner of Art so that fixation be obtained without poison, give an opportunity to the artificer to approach the Stone of Fire."

--Isaac Newton

The most common way of producing the Regulus begins with stibnite or the Kermes mineral.

Isaac Newton recommended two parts stibnite, one part of iron filings, and four parts of burnt tartar. The mixture is fused in a crucible and allowed to cool slowly.

A slag or scoria forms at the surface and easily comes off the metal with a hammer blow. Save this scoria from the first reduction of the ore to metal, it contains the *Seed of Gold*.

The metal or Regulus at the bottom of the crucible may show some signs of starring, but generally requires additional purification by grinding and fusion with niter to bring out the stars.

The use of iron in the reduction produces iron sulfide by taking the sulfur from the stibnite, leaving the antimony free as metal which sinks to the bottom.

Other methods of obtaining the Regulus include the use of niter in the mixture, For example, twelve parts stibnite, five parts iron filings, six parts niter, and nine parts raw tartar. Even small iron nails can be used for the reduction in place of iron filings.

The inclusion of raw tartar is said to increase the yield of the *Seed of Gold* in the scoria during the first fusion.

The exact proportions will depend on the quality of the stibnite you begin with.

A word of caution: the mixtures with niter are essentially a form of gunpowder which you will be placing into a very hot crucible. Add material slowly or you will soon find out why the ancients called this process *Detonation*.

The Regulus, once obtained, is ground and mixed with twice its weight of niter, then fused again in a crucible to purify it. This purification may be repeated several times in order for the starry qualities to develop in the metal. This **Star Regulus of Antimony** is also called the **Martial Regulus** because of the iron used in its production.

The Regulus has healing power of its own. An extraction of the powdered metal with spirit of turpentine turns a deep red. Removal of the turpentine leaves an oil which is dissolved into spirit of wine and used for all pulmonary illnesses. This is called the **Balm of Antimony**.

By far the greatest interest surrounding the Regulus is its fixed spirit or Mercury, which can be transferred to other metals in order to reanimate them and awaken their generative power. This path leads to confecting the Philosopher's Stone.

In one approach to this path, the **Martial Regulus** is alloyed with about twice as much pure silver and a small amount of copper to produce a **Lunar Venusian Regulus** which has a beautiful violet color.

This Regulus is then amalgamated with purified metallic mercury, washed and then distilled. The amalgamation and distillation is repeated seven to ten times and is referred to as **letting the eagles fly**. The Regulus of antimony will not amalgamate very easily with mercury metal, so the silver is added to absorb the fixed spirit of antimony and transfer it to the mercury.

The silver then, often called the **Doves of Diana**, acts as a medium to transfer the life force of the antimony into the mercury. After the distillation, the residue of silver which remains in the retort, called now the **Dead Doves of Diana**, is cleaned and used again. With each cycle of amalgamation and distillation, the mercury metal becomes more enlivened and ultimately is called **Animated Mercury**, containing the generative power of the metallic realm. It is the fertile field wherein the seed of metals is sown.

Purified gold metal is **seeded** into this animated mercury and digested over a long period. The matter will pass through a black stage, then gradually whiten and finally redden into the *ferment* or *Red Stone* which can be multiplied using fresh animated mercury.

The *Red Stone* forms the basis of the *Elixir* or *Universal Medicine for Man and Metals*. It also has the power to transmute the lesser metals into gold, but it must become dedicated to that purpose by a further process called *Inceration*, which we will talk about later. After this process, it serves only for transmutations of metal and not for medicinal use.

Another approach for using the Star Regulus to confect the stone, without the use of metallic mercury, unites the Regulus with gold through a long digestion with a menstruum, derived similarly to the urine alkahest, in a closed vessel.

The same progression of colors from black to white to red will be observed.

In this case, the Regulus is called the *Mercury* or *Our Luna* and the gold is called *Sol* or *Sulfur*. The liquid menstruum is also often referred to as *Mercury* to confuse you or is called the *Secret Fire*. It is the catalyst which unites the contrary metals. Thus you will often see pictures of the Sun and Moon being united by Mercury in alchemical works.

CHAPTER SIXTEEN

The Seed of Metals

"Matter is no other than a mere vapor, which extracted from the elementary earth by the superior stars, as by a sidereal distillation of the Macrocosm; which sidereal hot infusion, with any airy-sulfurous property descending upon inferiors, so acts and operates, that in those metals and minerals is implanted spiritually and invisibly a certain power and virtue, which fume afterwards resolves itself in the earth, into a certain water, from which mineral water all metals are thenceforth generated and ripened to their perfection; and thence proceeds this or that metal or mineral, according as one of the Three Principles acquires dominion."

-- Basil Valentine, "Triumphal Chariot of Antimony"

Today, products from the Mineral realm are not considered to have seeds or even to come from seeds, but in the works of alchemy, this is a great secret of the Art. Michael Sendivogius, in his "New Chemical Light" says:

"Nature is not visible, though she acts visibly; she is a volatile spirit who manifests herself in material shapes, and her existence is in the Will of God."

"She is One and produces different things but only through the mediate instrumentality of Seed."

"Nature performs whatsoever the Sperm requires of Her. Nature works on Seed."

Recall from above that Sendivogius called Seed, the Quintessence of a thing -- *its most perfect digestion and decoction* or the **Radical Moisture**. He further states that there is only one seed and that their difference is only caused by the place (the Womb) and degree of coction, but it is perfectly ripened in gold.

The "Collectanea Chemica" published around 1650, describes it thus:

> "The seed of metals is what the Sons of Wisdom have called their Mercury, to distinguish it from quicksilver, which it nearly resembles, being the Radical Moisture of metals. This, when judiciously extracted, without corrosives, or fluxing, contains in it a seminal quality whose perfect ripeness is only in gold; in the other metals it is crude, like fruits which are yet green, not being sufficiently digested by the heat of the Sun and action of the elements, We observed that the Radical Moisture contains the Seed, which is true; yet it is not the Seed, but the Sperm only, in which the Vital Principle floats, being invisible to the eye."

> "Though the seed is the most glorious of all created things, yet the womb is its life, which causes the putrefaction of the enclosing grain or sperm, brings about the congelation of the Vital Atom, nourishing and stimulating its growth by the warmth of its own body."

The Salt or body *determines* the Fire or Seed to *burn* in a characteristic manner here in the physical world. Salt is the Womb wherein the Sulfurous nature and the Mercurial nature unite to produce the *Living Chemical Child* in which the Celestial Fire incarnates.

Everything produces seed after its own nature and so the sages often remind us that the proper seed placed into the proper matrix is the work of the artist, and then Nature takes over and is all too happy to bring the material to fruition. The sages tell us that you won't get a dog by planting a wheat seed nor a cow from a hen's egg, so do not expect to grow any metal without the Metallic Seed.

So where do we find the seeds of metals? The "Collectanea Chemica" tells us quite plainly and naturally that the seed of metals is found in their ore just as they occur in nature. Certainly then, the most coveted seed is the *Seed of Gold* as gold contains the most perfect reflection of the Celestial Fire.

> "The Stone you seek, we said and still affirm is only gold, brought to so high perfection as it is possible, which though a firm compacted body is, yet by art's direction, and nature's operation, made a tinging spirit which will never fade."

> -- Philalethes

Just as the alchemists describe many *Degrees of Fire*, so do they also describe many *Grades of Gold* and we must often discern which gold they are speaking of.

> "In order that you may desire nothing that belongs to the theory and practice of our Philosophy, I will tell you that, according to Philosophers, there are three kinds of Gold."

> "The first one is an Astral Gold, whose center is in the Sun, which with its rays communicates it, at the same time as its light, to all heavenly bodies under it. It is an

igneous substance, and a continuous emanation of solar corpuscles which, being in a perpetual flux and reflux, because of the movement of the sun and the stars, fills up the whole universe. Everything is penetrated by this Gold in the immensity of heavens upon earth, and, in its bowels, we breathe continuously this Astral Gold, the solar particles penetrate our bodies and are ceaselessly exhaled from them.

"The second one is an Elemental Gold, that is, the purest and most fixed portion of the elements, and of all substances composed by them; so that every sub lunar being of the three genera contains in its center a precious grain of this Elemental Gold.

"The third one is the handsome metal, whose brightness and inalterable perfection give it a price, which make it to be considered by all men as the sovereign remedy for all evils and needs of life, and as the only foundation of greatness and human power."

-- "The Hermetical Triumph"

Another early writer describes the Astral Gold thus:

"It is a Universal Fluid, a living one, extended throughout all Nature, which penetrates all beings; it is the most subtle of all things, incorruptible in its essence, and permeating the infinite space. The sun and planets are but condensed states of this Universal Principle, distributing their abundances through their palpitating hearts, and sending them to the forms of the lower worlds and to every being, acting through their own centers, and impelling those forms to a higher state in the path of perfection. This spirit may be obtained in the same way as it is communicated to earth from the stars. The forms in which this living principle becomes fixed, become perfect and permanent. Thus, the Philosophical Stone is the

154

ultimate that can be made using it, making that which is volatile to become fixed."

-- Johannes Trithemius

"The gold of the wise is proper the gold of the second species; for, when this gold is perfectly calcinated, and exalted to the cleanness and whiteness of snow, it acquires, by Magistery, a natural sympathy for the Astral Gold, of whom it has become visibly a true magnet, it attracts and concentrates in itself so great a quantity of Astral Gold and of solar particles, received from the continuous emanation of them done in the center of the Sun and Moon, that it is in a disposition near to become the living gold of the Philosophers."

-- "Hermetical Triumph"

CHAPTER SEVENTEEN

The Philosopher's Stone

According to Hermetic tradition, the Philosopher's Stone is manifest as a heavy crystalline substance which is described as being quite similar to pulverized glass, ranging from crimson to saffron in color.

It has no odor, is not combustible and yet melts easily like wax by candle flame alone and readily dissolves into water or wine. The materials to make it are abundant and to be had by anyone.

The Stone is said to have the power to cure all sickness, give back lost youth, and to transmute other metals into gold.

The old Adepts constantly assure us of its physical reality. There are exhibits in several European Museums, which are reportedly alchemically made gold. Even up to our current times, reports of successful transmutations are found.

Near the end of the nineteenth century, alchemical transmutation was considered a dead issue. "The elements are immutable." Then came the discovery of radioactivity and the fact that transmutation of elements was occurring naturally.

In the 1960s it was announced that the alchemist's dream had been realized when scientists formed a tiny amount of gold by bombarding a pool of mercury with high energy particles.

In the 1970s and 1980s the work of the French biochemist Louis Kervran revealed the possibility of elemental transmutation as a natural process in living systems and gave it the name **Biological Transmutations**.

Today the controversy over **Cold Fusion** is still in progress, and **Quantum Physics** tells us the observer has an effect on the material world. The promises of alchemy seem to be far from a dead issue.

The perfection and evolution of the alchemist is the true goal in all of this. We mentioned that one must become the living stone before being able to produce the tangible stone.

The skills necessary for its production and the way to proceed are gradually revealed to the alchemist as his own transformation unfolds. The actual physical stone is regarded more as a final test or proof that he has been successful, although at that point the transmutation of base metals to gold will become a trivial pursuit.

In the wrong hands the Stone could have a devastating effect on the world economy for the Stone could be made to multiply, not only in quantity but in transforming power, where an ounce could produce ten thousand ounces of gold and cure hundreds of people at Death's door.

As Christopher Glaser wrote in his Chemical textbook about 1650 -- Would you ever feel safe walking down the street knowing that in your vest pocket lay the potential to create ten thousand ounces of gold? In the past, many were imprisoned and tortured to reveal the secrets of making gold. Do you think it would be any different today?

Some say this is the reason why alchemy has been such a closely guarded secret by the adepts. How does that go? "With great power comes great responsibility and the ability to attract great consequences."

> "Therefore the philosophers say their matter is in all things, yet have selected such subjects wherein the Universal Spirit is more abundantly contained and more concentrated and easier to be obtained."
>
> -- "Golden Chain of Homer"

Divine Cinnabar

We've mentioned two of the commonly used paths for confecting the Philosopher's Stone, that of the *Wet Way* through lead acetate, and the *Dry Way* through the *Star Regulus of Antimony*.

The final method we examine is often called the way of the *Divine Cinnabar*. I saved this for last because it is a dangerous operation requiring the use of the very toxic metallic mercury. The other two methods also present dangers and the use of toxic materials, but mercury is particularly insidious and can quickly contaminate an area which will then be very difficult to clean up.

Some alchemists avoid working with mercury metal altogether because of the danger to themselves and those around them. The use of metallic mercury is well established in both Chinese and Indian alchemy as well.

All of the laboratory skills you have developed in the *Lesser Works* will be called into play in these works -- *The Great Work*-- in order to avoid mishap. More than one alchemist has lost his life in this work, so be cautious and *Know the theory first before attempting the praxis.*

Metallic mercury or *common* mercury is a curious thing, liquid at normal temperatures, bright like silver and heavy like gold. It seems poised to become any of the other metals. The slightest vibration sets it quivering for some time. It seems alive.

The ancients called it *Argent Vive*, living silver, or *Quicksilver* because it is always quick to move, but also because it is easily *quickened* with life. Being in the liquid state, mercury is still heavily influenced by the subtle spiritual energies around it.

The basic idea behind the mercury work is that the mercury plays the part of the female and gold is the male, their proper union results in the birth of *The Chemical Child* -- the Philosopher's Stone.

Of course not just any old mercury and gold metals will work, they need *Philosophical* preparation. The mercury must be purified before work can begin. Then the purified mercury is reanimated or recharged with Universal Fire to awaken its generative power. The *Animated Mercury* is then digested with prepared gold in the proper proportion and regimen of heat until it passes through the black, white, and finally to the red stage or *Red Stone*. Much the same as with the Star Regulus of Antimony mentioned earlier.

> "Gold is the true leaven of the Elixir. Marriage will take place between the mercury menstruum (the female), and the Sun/gold (the male). The woman is said to draw the sperm or "seed" of the gold. The seed of the noble metal will make the mercury like itself through digestion alone"

> -- Lintaut, "Friend of the Dawn", circa 1700

Purification of Mercury Metal

We can buy high purity mercury (triple distilled) from the chemical supply store, but it is still a good idea to purify it in the old ways. It is not so much aimed at getting the mercury any more pure, than exalting it alchemically and opening the body to receive new life.

For this, take your mercury and wash it well with rainwater, then squeeze it through a piece of chamois or some other thin pliable leather.

Now cover the mercury with dried and powdered sea salt. Mix these two completely using a mortar and pestle. Depending on the impurities in the mercury, the salt may darken even to blackness. Wash this dirty salt out using rainwater and repeat the salt washing once or twice. The mercury will retain some of the subtle essence of the salt which is important for the rest of the processes.

Put the mercury into a mortar and add an equal amount of sea salt. Saturate this mixture with strong distilled vinegar (about 10% acetic acid) and begin vigorously mixing the mass for about ten minutes. Now wash this salt out with rainwater

160

until the mercury appears shiny and bright. Press it through a chamois. There should be no residue left in the chamois. The mercury should leave no trail when rolled across a smooth surface and should be without any appearance of scum at the surface. This mercury is now "the field prepared and fit to receive our noble king."

Animation of the Mercury

Animation is described as the addition of etheric essences or principles in the etheric shell of a substance and awakening its generative virtue.

There are many ways to animate mercury. We mentioned the most popular method earlier when discussing *The Flamel Path* with the *Star Regulus of Antimony.*

The simplest method is to use native gold alone with the purified mercury. Use a form of pure native gold such as gold nuggets or gold dust as obtained by panning in a river. The gold is reduced to a powder by grinding with salt and vinegar into a paste. Wash out the salt and let the gold dry. To twenty nine parts of purified mercury, add 1 1/4 parts of gold powder and grind them into a fluid amalgam. Wash the amalgam with water until it is clean and bright. Wipe the surface with a piece of paper towel until dry, then place the dried amalgam into a tall, strong glass vessel and seal it well. Let this matter digest at about 40°C for three months. After three months, increase the temperature to 60°C and continue digestion for another three months.

> "This action stirs up the hidden power in the mercury, which, totally surrounding the noble metal, gradually dissolves it, releasing its power into the dissolving menstruum."

> "The mercury starts to acquire the subtle seed of the noble metal, thus being animated."

> -- Lintaut, "Friend of the Dawn", circa 1700

161

The result of this six month digestion is **_Animated Mercury_**. Be sure to make a sufficient quantity of this because the later operations of multiplication and augmentation of the Stone will require it. This method of animation requires time (six months), but the manipulation of hazardous materials is kept to a minimum.

The final method of mercury animation we will examine is the way of the **_Divine Cinnabar._** This process requires a great deal of care as it is quite dangerous, but is held to be one of the most powerful ways to animate metallic mercury and produce the Philosophical Stone.

We begin with metallic mercury purified with salt and vinegar as above. Mix the mercury with an equal amount of native sulfur in a mortar, grinding it together well. The matter will turn black during this process, forming mercury sulfide. Examine the matter closely with a magnifier. There should be no tiny globules of mercury remaining. Grind with additional sulfur if there are.

The resulting black mass is a crude form of cinnabar, which is the sulfide ore of mercury. We can proceed with the black variety of cinnabar or we can improve this matter by sublimation to obtain the beautiful orange variety of cinnabar which is best, but difficult and dangerous to perform.

Now mix the cinnabar (black or orange) with an equal weight of iron filings and place this into a strong retort for distillation. As with the Star Regulus of Antimony, the iron will take up the sulfur from the cinnabar. Mercury metal will be reduced and begin to distil over. Some operators recommend using a 50 / 50 mixture of Star Regulus and iron filings for this distillation. In both cases, it is the subtle essence obtained from the iron itself that is the key.

> "The red, solar, sulfureous principle of iron (or its counterpart in regulus of antimony) acts on the mercury with increasing force each operation."
>
> -- Lintaut, "Friend of the Dawn," 1700

The outlet of the distillation is led into a container of water where the mercury vapor is condensed into a pool of bright shining mercury metal. The reaction can become quite vigorous so careful heating and strong vessels are required as is proper ventilation.

An easy way to perform the distillations of mercury amalgam is to construct a small retort using iron pipe fittings from the hardware store, pack charcoal briquettes around it and start the fire outside. Again the outlet is submerged in a container of water and the distillation of metallic mercury proceeds. When the distillation stops, be sure to remove the retort outlet from the water or the vacuum created by the cooling retort will draw the water into the apparatus with possible dire consequences, i.e. explosion.

Collect all of the mercury that distills and squeeze it through a chamois, and this will conclude one cycle or *Eagle*. The process of making cinnabar with fresh native sulfur and its reduction by distillation with iron is repeated on this mercury until *seven Eagles have flown*.

It is not that the mercury gets any more purified during this process, but its inner etheric shell of sulfurous and mercurial principles is activated. After the final Eagle, distill the mercury two times by itself. This results in an Animated Mercury.
"It is the fertilized matrix in which you may plant your corn."

The Alchemical Rebis

Once we have a supply of Animated Mercury from one of the above methods, or from the Star Regulus of Antimony method, the next step is to form the so-called *Rebis* wherein the opposites are united.

Take four parts of your Animated Mercury and carefully amalgamate it with one part of fine gold powder in a glass mortar. Wash the amalgam with water until it is clean and shining then blot it dry with a cloth.

Place the cleaned amalgam into a long-necked glass vessel so that only a third of it is filled. This should be made of strong glass and able to seal very tightly.

Now warm the entire vessel and contents to about 50°C and quickly seal it air tight and allow it to cool a bit. In the old days this is where the **Hermetic Seal** would be applied by heating the neck of the vessel and melting it closed. Today glassware is available with precision ground joints and is sufficiently air tight for this.

The sealed vessel is now set to digest at about 40° to 50°C. After about three months at this heat, the matter will begin to darken and finally turn black. This is the so-called **Nigredo** phase or **Black Stage**.

Once the matter is entirely black, gently raise the heat to about 60° to 65°C and continue the digestion. After two to three months the matter will acquire an iridescence at the surface with colors reminiscent of a **Peacock's Tail**, which is what the adepts called this stage. As the digestion continues, the matter will gradually become lighter marking the beginning of the **Albedo** stage or Whitening.

It will take about nine more months for the matter to become entirely white. When this happens, the heat is very slowly raised to about 130°C over the course of several months.

The whiteness gradually gives way to a yellowness that deepens with time into red. This is the **Rubedo** stage or **Red Stage** of the Stone. Once this point is reached, the matter should be digested at about 200°C for an additional two months in order to mature.

Allow the matter to slowly cool, then break the vessel to remove the contents which is the **Red Stone** in the First Degree.

Inceration

In order to effect metallic transmutations, the Red Stone must undergo some further processing. Once this happens the Stone is no longer used for medicine but is solely dedicated to the purpose of transmutation.

This final processing is called **Inceration**, which means to make something like wax. Inceration augments the Stone's fusibility and ingress into metals -- that is, its ability to penetrate.

Begin this by grinding a portion of the Red Stone to a powder and then amalgamate it with six times its weight of Animated Mercury. Wash the amalgam with rain water several times, then blot it dry with a cloth.

Squeeze the dried amalgam through a chamois and save aside the mercury that passes through the chamois for later use.

Collect the soft amalgam from inside the chamois and place into a tall glass vessel as before.

The matter is now digested for three months at each of the four heats used in preparing the Red Stone, (i.e., 40, 65, 130, 200°C).

At the end of the digestion, break open the vessel and remove the matter which should now be easy to fuse like wax and not smoke at all.

The Red Stone prepared in this way is now suitable for *Projection* on metals.

Multiplication of the Red Stone

The Red Stone in the First Degree is said to have the power to transmute metals in the ratio of one part Stone to ten parts metal. The Stone's power can be increased ten-fold in a process called *Multiplication*. This process is very much like that of preparing the original Red Stone, only it takes much less time.

Take one part of the Red Stone in the First Degree, and amalgamate it with ten parts Animated Mercury. Wash the amalgam with rainwater then blot it dry.
Place the clean amalgam into a tall glass vessel and seal as before. Now begin the same regimen of heating and digestion starting at 40°C.

The matter will undergo the same series of color changes, (i.e., black, white and finally red) but in a much shorter time. Increase the heat according to the color changes as before.

After the Red Stage has been reached, the matter is cooled and removed from the vessel. Its power is now such that one part will act on one hundred parts of metal.

If we take this Red Stone and repeat the process of multiplication on it, one part will act on one thousand parts of metal, then ten thousand parts, and so on.

Remember that before the Stone can be used for metallic transmutations it must go through the process of *Inceration*, whatever degree it has been multiplied to.

Some believe it is quite dangerous to multiply the Stone more than seven times, as it is said to become first luminous then unstable altogether with the possibility of catastrophic consequences.

Projection

The final test of the Stone and proof that the operator has worked correctly, is the transmutation of metals.

Projection is the term used to describe the addition of the *Perfected Solar Medicine* to molten metals by *projecting* it on top of the melted matter in a crucible, resulting in its transmutation.

Depending on the quality and multiplication of the Stone, more or less of it may be required to effect the transmutation of various metals. For example, if one part of the stone is found to act on one hundred parts of pure silver, that same one part may only affect ten parts of a more crude metal such as tin or lead.

Silver is a noble metal next to gold and often used as a guide in determining the strength of the Red Stone's power to effect transmutation.

Let us say that we have the Red Stone multiplied to a strength of one part to one hundred parts metal. Take one hundred parts of pure silver metal and melt it in a crucible. When it is completely molten, take one part of the Incerated Red Stone and form it into several small balls or pills. Slowly add one pill at a time to the crucible and allow it to fuse with the silver. Continue adding the small pills until you have added the full one part.

Keep the contents molten for an additional two hours as the metal matures and evolves.

At the end of the two hours, allow the matter to cool slowly and then break it from the crucible.

Now re-melt the metal and cast it into an ingot. All of the silver should have changed to 24k gold. An assay of the metal may reveal the presence of silver which did not change, so the strength of the Stone can be determined at, say 180 to 1 instead of the expected 200 to 1. On the contrary, a portion of the metal may be melted with additional pure silver and reveal that it has strength to transmute even more than expected, say 300 to 1.

This assessment of the Stone's power will allow you to judge the proper amount to effect the transmutation desired and yet not waste this most precious of medicines.

The Elizabethan scholar / physician Dr. John Dee and his alchemist associate, Edward Kelly, are said to have learned a painful lesson in this. Having come into possession of a quantity of the Red Stone, they proceeded to make various transmutations only to discover later that the power of the Stone was far greater than they had imagined. Unfortunately they did not realize this until more than half of the Stone had been used up.

CONCLUSION

O ther chemists I meet often ask me, "Is alchemy like chemistry?" To which, I usually reply, "No, not at all really."

Alchemy and chemistry parted ways centuries ago and not under the best of terms. Over time, laboratory alchemy became even more obscured by the new terminology and goals of the developing science of modern chemistry. Most chemists today do not have a clue as to what alchemy is really about. The subject has had such a stigma placed on it from medieval times that much of its potential remains unexplored.

Modern science has come a long way in the exploration of Nature, still it is not all-knowing. Around the turn of the twentieth century, science reveled in the discovery of *its three essential* building blocks of matter (the proton, neutron, and electron) under the influence of *the four fundamental forces*. Later on, the fundamental particles themselves were found to be composed of a whole cornucopia of smaller particles and some of these smaller particles were composed of yet smaller particles. It seems to go on and on but we've reached some limitations in divisibility or in the determination of division and it becomes a tangle of statistics and probabilities. Interestingly enough, the powers of mind begin to reveal themselves and the observer becomes a key issue. At this *Quantum* level of subtle matter, modern science recognizes the influence of mind. It also recognizes various modalities in time and space like sheets or layers or *spheres* of being. It is starting to sound a bit like *Jabir-ish*.

We mentioned earlier that science is coming full circle to that which was taught in the ancient mystery schools.

Even modern medical science is beginning to recognize man's subtle energy substructure such as the acupuncture meridians.

Practical alchemy has labored under a bad reputation, branded fraud or at best pseudo-science by those with no practical experience in the matter at all.

There are many secrets still hidden in the ancient Art waiting to be rediscovered by the practicing artist. As the alchemist known as Magophon said, "The disciple must exert himself to realize all his concepts."

You have to do the work in order for the light to shine, Nature will do Her part.

The well known occult writer, Israel Regardie, published a book entitled *The Philosopher's Stone* in 1938, wherein he examines alchemy from several mystical and psychological points of view. Later in life, he became a student of Frater Albertus at the Paracelsus Research Society, which "opened his eyes." In his introduction to the second edition of the book, he had this to say regarding his experience of laboratory alchemy:

> "It took no more than a few minutes to help me realize how presumptuous I had been to assert dogmatically that all alchemy was psycho-spiritual. What I witnessed there and have since repeated, has sufficed to enable me to state categorically that, in insisting solely on a mystical interpretation of alchemy, I had done a grave disservice to the ancient sages and philosophers."

There is only the One Thing, *The Celestial Fire*, and we all have a part to play on its journey of self-realization. The Great Work is about following Nature and helping Nature in this unfoldment. The Celestial Fire is often termed *The Divine Will*. Our own Will is the reflection of this Fire which drives all of creation.

Discovering our True Will or Purpose and fulfilling that purpose is the highest accomplishment of the alchemist and service to Nature.

> "The secret of alchemy is this; there is a way of manipulating matter and energy so as to produce what modern scientists call a "field of force." This field acts on the observer and places him in a privileged position within the universe. From this position he has access to the realities which are ordinarily hidden from us by time and space, energy and matter. This is what we call "The Great Work."
>
> -- Fulcanelli

Appendix

TABLE ONE

PLANET	METAL	ORGAN	WEEKDAY
Sun	Gold	Heart	Sunday
Moon	Silver	Brain	Monday
Mars	Iron	Gall	Tuesday
Mercury	Mercury	Lungs	Wednesday
Jupiter	Tin	Liver	Thursday
Venus	Copper	Kidneys	Friday
Saturn	Lead	Spleen	Saturday

Appendix

TABLE TWO

Herbs And Planets

This table is just a short selection of common herbs and their planetary rulers. Most of these associations are taken from the 16th century herbalist Nicholas Culpepper's, "Compleat Herbal," held in esteem by a number of alchemists old and modern.

SUN: *angelica, bay, chamomile, celandine, eyebright, juniper, marigold, rosemary, rue, saffron, St. John's wort, sundew, walnut*

MOON: *chickweed, cleavers, watercress, cucumber, lettuce, water-lily, moonwort, wallflower, willow*

MERCURY: *wild carrot, caraway, dill, hazelnut, horehound, lavender, lily, liquorice, marjoram, oats, parsley, parsnip, savory, honeysuckle, valerian*

VENUS: *burdock, columbine, coltsfoot, daisy, eringo, featherfew, figwort, goldenrod, marshmallow, mint, mother-wort, mugwort, catnip, pennyroyal, plantain, periwinkle, poppy, purslane, primrose, strawberry, yarrow*

MARS: *all-heal, barberry, basil, garlic, gentian, hawthorn, hops, nettle, onion, radish, rhubarb, tobacco, wormwood*

JUPITER: *Melissa, bilberry, borage, chervil, cinquefoil, dandelion, dock, endive, hyssop, house-leek, melilot, oak, roses*

SATURN: amaranthus, barley, corn, beet, comfrey, dodder, elm, fumitory, horsetail, holly, ivy, mullein, nightshade, shepherd's-purse, blackthorn, woad, wintergreen, yew

BIBLIOGRAPHY

Most of the works cited in this book, and a great deal more, are available in various translations on the Internet. Two of my favorite places for original texts are http://www.levity.com/alchemy and http://www.alchemylab.com.

Allen, Paul M., ed. "Secret Symbols of the Rosicrucians of the 16th and 17th Centuries" in *A Christian Rosenkreutz Anthology*. New York: Rudolf Steiner Publications, 1968.

Anonymous. *Collectanea Chemica*, From the 1893 James Elliot & Co. First Edition. London: Vincent Stuart Publishers LTD, 1963.

Anonymous *Praxis Spagyrica Philosophica*, English translation from the original 1711 German Edition with commentary by Frater Albertus. Salt Lake City, Utah: Paracelsus Research Society, 1966.

Altus. *Mutus Liber*, first published at La Rochelle in 1677. French edition with commentary by Magophon, translated by Kjell Hellesoe. Stavenger, 1985.

Becker, Christian August. *Das Acetone*. 1867. Translated by Shuck and Nintzel, Richardson, Texas: Restorers of Alchemical Manuscripts. 1981.

De Lintaut, Henri. *Friend of the Dawn* 1700 edition translated by Wilson Wheatcroft, India. Richardson, Texas: Restorers of Alchemical Manuscripts, 1982.

Della Porta, Jean Baptiste. *Natural Magic*, Book Ten. New York: 1585. Basic Books, 1957.

Dobbs, B.J.T., *The Foundations of Newton's Alchemy*. Cambridge: Cambridge University Press, 1975.

Dubuis, Jean. *PON Seminars1992*. Translated by Patrice Maleze. Winfield, Illinois: The Philosophers of Nature, 1992.

Essentia: Journal of Evolutionary Thought in Action. Salt Lake City, Utah: Quarterly publication of Paracelsus College, 1980.

Flamel, Nicholas. *Hieroglyphical Figures*. Translated by Eirenaeus Orandus for Thomas Walsley, at the Eagle and Child in Britans Burusse. London: 1624.

Frater Albertus. *Alchemist's Handbook*. Salt Lake City, Utah: Paracelsus Research Society, 1974.

French, John. *The Art of Distillation*. Original 1651 edition published in London. San Francisco, CA: Para Publishers, 1978.

Fulcanelli. *The Dwellings of The Philosophers*. Translated by Donvez and Perrin. Boulder, CO: Archive Press and Communications, 1999.

Glauber, Johann Rudolf. *The Complete Works of Rudolf Glauber*. Translated by Christopher Packe. Boulder, CO 1983.

Glaser, Christopher. *The Complete Chymist*. 1677. Richardson, Texas: Restorers of Alchemical Manuscripts,1983.

Hartmann, Franz. *The Life of Paracelsus*. Los Angeles, California: Mokulume Hill Press 1972

Hauck, Dennis William. *The Emerald Tablet: Alchemy for Personal Transformation*. New York: Penguin, 1999.

Holland, Isaac. A *Compendium of Writings by Johan Isaaci Hollandus*. Translated from German by RAMS. Richardson, Texas: Restorers of Alchemical Manuscripts, 1981.

Hurley, Phillip. *Herbal Alchemy*. Lotus Publications, 1977.

Junius, Manfred M. *The Practical Handbook of Plant Alchemy*. New York: Inner Traditions, 1985.

Kervran, Louis. *Biological Transmutations*. London: Crosby Lockwood, 1972.

Kirschweger, Anton. *The Golden Chain of Homer*. Translated from the German 1723 edition by Sigmund Bacstrom in 1797. (Xerox of Bacstrom's handwritten copy.)

Murien, Petri. *Alchemically Purified and Solidified Mercury*. Translated by Brigitte Donvez. La-Screen. Rasa Vidya Marg, India: Chinchwad, 1992.

Newton, Isaac. *Keynes Ms 64*, King's College Library, University of Cambridge.

Paracelsus. *The Hermetic and Alchemical Writings of Paracelsus*, edited by Arthur Edward Waite. Reprint of the 1894 edition published by James Elliot & Co., London. University Books Inc., 1967.

Paracelsus. *Volumen Medicinae Paramirum*. Translated from the original German by Kurt F. Leidecker. Baltimore: The Johns Hopkins Press, 1949.

Philalethes, Eirenaeus. *An Open Entrance to the Closed Palace of the King*. Richardson, Texas: Restorers of Alchemical Manuscripts 1981.

Regardie, Israel. *The Philosopher's Stone*, 2nd Edition. St. Paul, Minnesota: Llewellyn Publications, 1970.

Ripley, George. *Liber Secretisimuss*. Richardson, Texas: Restorers of Alchemical Manuscripts, 1982.

Sendivogius, Michael. *The New Chemical Light*. First published in 1608.

Richardson, Texas: Restorers of Alchemical Manuscripts, 1982.

The Hermetical Triumph. Printed for Thomas Harris, at the Looking-Glas and Bible, on London Bridge. 1723.

Three Initiates. *Kybalion* Chicago: The Yogi Publication Society, 1922.

Trismegistus, Hermes. *Golden Tractate of Hermes*. Salt Lake City, Utah: Para Publishing Co. Inc., 1973.

Valentine, Basil. *Triumphant Chariot of Antimony* with annotations of Theodore Kirkringius MD. Printed for Dorman Newman at the Kings Arms in the Poultry, 1678. Photocopy of original edition.

Weidenfeld, Johannes Segerus. *Secrets of the Adepts*. 1685. Richardson, Texas: Restorers of Alchemical Manuscripts, 1982.

Way of the Crucible
Real Alchemy for Real Alchemists

Robert Allen Bartlett

This book is the next step in your Alchemical Studies. *The Way of the Crucible* provides directions for a more advanced understanding of the mineral work. It is a ground-breaking modern manual on the art of Alchemy that draws on both modern scientific technology and ancient methods.

Bartlett provides an overview of how practical alchemy works, along with an exploration of the theories behind its practice. The author also explains what the ancients really meant when they used the term "Philosopher's Stone" and describes practical methods toward its achievement. Includes treatises on Astrology, Qabalah, Herbalism, and minerals, as they relate to Alchemy

Robert Allen Bartlett has been a practicing alchemist for over thirty years and was a student of the twentieth century's most highly recognized alchemist, Frater Albertus, at Paracelsus College. After receiving his degree in Chemistry, Bartlett was appointed Chief Chemist at Frater Albertus' Paralab. He is a member of the International Alchemy Guild at the Adept Level. He is an Instructor in Spagyrics at Flamel College Online through www.Alchemylab.com

Paperback • $22.95 • 6 x 9 • 332 pages
Numerous illustrations • ISBN: 978-0-89254-154-6

Design, typesetting and diagrams
by William J. Kiesel
www . bookarts . org
Cover illustration rendered
by Benjamin Vierling
www . bvierling . com